IF GOD IS SO GOOD, WHY ARE BLACKS DOING SO BAD?

To: Shelton
Be All God made
you to be! Amazing!

JAMES DIXON, II

IF GOD IS SO GOOD,
WHY ARE BLACKS DOING SO BAD?
Copyright © 2011 by James Dixon, II

ISBN: 0-9786581-7-5
978-0-9786581-7-5

Published by

LIFEBRIDGE
BOOKS
P.O. BOX 49428
CHARLOTTE, NC 28277

Printed in the United States of America.

DEDICATION

*To those who sacrificed before us; to those
who labor among us; to those to come who
depend on us...I dedicate this work.*

ACKNOWLEDGMENTS

*I must openly declare my abundant appreciation
to the plethora of persons without whom this work
would have remained an idea, an intellectual
fetus that never would have been birthed.*

*I am grateful for the prayers and push given by my
family during this project. Thank you to my wife, Tanisha,
our daughters, Mariah and Victoria, and son, James III.
God's grace to me through each of you is without measure.*

*Many thanks to the team of persons who typed, read,
edited, challenged, and advised. Crystal Jackson, your
"any hour" devotion is unmatched. Community of Faith,
thank you for believing in me and hearing me. I am
energized by your endless encouragement.*

Ultimately, TO GOD BE THE GLORY!

QUICK QUOTES OF CONFIDENCE

"I am proud that from my district has come this powerful message of love and liberation. Bishop Dixon is a leader for our times."
– CONGRESSWOMAN SHEILA JACKSON LEE

"This book addresses the crisis of anti-intellectualism and challenges a generation to change its course."
– DR. ROD PAIGE, FORMER U.S. SECRETARY OF EDUCATION

"If W.E.B. Dubois identified the "color line" as being the problem of the twentieth century, Bishop Dixon's must-read book has raised the critical question of the 21st century. This book challenges that pathos in the black community and tells it like it is. It's not for the faint of faith."
– JAMES T. CAMPBELL, HOUSTON CHRONICLE COLUMNIST

"Every African American, especially athletes should read this. I watched my friend write it. I have seen him live it."
– AVERY JOHNSON, HEAD COACH, DALLAS MAVERICKS

"Solving the problem of crime and incarceration is paramount for black America. This book hits the nail on the head."
– DR. LEE P. BROWN, FORMER U.S. DRUG CZAR

"A must read: This author speaks truth to power!"
– DEBRA FRASER-HOWZE, PRESIDENT, NATIONAL BLACK LEADERSHIP COMMISSION ON AIDS

"From the street corners in our community, to the halls of Congress, this book makes sense."
- CONGRESSMAN ALEXANDER GREEN

"This book is capable of liberating blacks from internal tyranny and fortifying them from external terror."
- BISHOP NOEL JONES

FOREWORD

This book should be read by everybody. It deals with the situation of African Americans in the United States, but its issues are multicultural, and relevant to all of our society. Its very title is engaging, crafted with black preacher skill like the title of a sermon. But it is hardly sermonic.

In the ten very readable chapters of this book, Bishop Dixon has pointed at the several tributaries of the problem of the black community. One might expect an inner city pastor, born and reared in a low-income neighborhood, to begin such a work with a diatribe about the injustices of institutional racism. Bishop Dixon does not deny this. But he carries us beyond the outside sores of racial discrimination to inner cancers of generational separation, a loss of interest in learning, a growing obsession with material "bling bling," a massive overpopulation of jails and prisons with blacks—males and females—and an economic segregation within our own community, pitting black "haves" against black "have nots."

The author makes it clear that what the Anglo establishment is doing to us as a people is minimal compared to what we are doing to ourselves as we first ignore, then discard the values of faith, family and hard work which we inherited from our elders.

Bishop Dixon cites the heroes and heroines of our history, reminds us of the massive obstacles they faced and overcame, and that our faith has always led to triumphs despite whatever deterioration we had allowed. And he ends the book with a hard-hitting 32-point program of things we can do to improve conditions within our own community.

This book should be required reading in secondary schools and colleges, in churches, for parents and grandparents, and for successful professional African Americans who need to be persuaded to mentor, to volunteer, to contribute, to give back. If God can raise up an obstreperous Israel, He can cure what ails us—if we let Him use us.

– Rev. William A. Lawson, Founder-Pastor Emeritus,
Wheeler Avenue Church, Houston, TX

CONTENTS

SOUND THE ALARM

The date was September 8; the year was 1900. What happened this dreadful day would become an unforgettable horror in Texas history. A violent hurricane struck Galveston Island destroying industry, taking the lives of 8,000 men, women and children and ruining the future of a city—a thriving community previously labeled by the *New York Herald* as the *New York of the Gulf.*

Today, when most people think of Texas, the cities of Houston, Dallas, Austin or San Antonio quickly come to mind. But before the Storm of 1900, Galveston was in first place, followed by Houston, located 50 miles north. It's hard to believe that Houston ran second place and Galveston was the city to watch on the Gulf Coast.

All of this forever changed on that September day in 1900. The hurricane carrying winds of over 140 miles per hour, created a storm surge of over 15 feet which literally drowned the city; killing, destroying and permanently altering its course and relegating it to the margins of U.S. history.

For years, questions—haunting questions—have loomed concerning pre-storm preparations and the decisions and actions of those responsible for public preparedness and safety under such conditions. Why wasn't a call issued for mass evacuation? Why were so many people trapped in the deluge that would become the liquid grave of thousands? Why did so many appear completely calm until it was too late to respond to the apparent emergency? What would Galveston, Texas, be today had those in positions of responsibility taken precautions and given adequate instructions for residents to evacuate before the storm became a weapon of mass destruction?

THE IMPENDING TRAGEDY

The similarities of the catastrophic storm, which pillaged Galveston at the turn of the last century and the impending storm I am convinced is headed for black America, are startling and stirring. In both instances, the masses suffer as a result of the blatant irresponsibility of an elite few—those empowered to lead.

Erik Larson, in his bestseller *Isaac's Storm*, provides a historical account of the Galveston hurricane which mirrors the plight of the African American people. His report captures and declares the tragedy that can and will likely occur when the hubris of mere mortals collides with the strength of nature.

At the center of Larson's chronicle is Isaac Cline, who was stationed on Galveston Island as the Chief of the U. S. Weather Service. Although he would be passionately appealed to by his younger brother and assistant, Joseph, he held to a position that would prove deadly. Under the influence of immense intellectual pride and the gross downplay of the storm's strength by the National Weather Service, he would choose not to sound the alarm announcing that the approaching storm would be a definite killer.

William Moore, the National Bureau's Director who abhorred the word "hurricane," sent a telegraph to Isaac classifying the threatening conditions as nothing more than a tropical storm. Isaac, who believed himself to fully comprehend the subject of "weather," had earlier written an article in 1893 dispelling all suspicion Galveston Island could one day be destroyed by storm waters. After conducting critical analyses, he concluded that Galveston's topography prevented such a possibility; even though earlier storms had repeatedly flooded the city.

It was this previous study upon which Isaac based his decision to advise the Corps of Engineers against erecting a seawall to protect the citizens. According to Isaac, the trusted expert, the expense of construction was unwarranted. It is believed however that at least part of his motivation was to allay fears which would have slowed investments in Galveston, giving Houston an edge in the race to become the leading port on the Gulf.

In his 1891 article, after appraising the city's storm readiness, Isaac wrote… *"The opinion held by some who are unacquainted with the actual condition of things, that Galveston will at some time be seriously damaged by some such disturbance is simply an absurd delusion."*

Even with the persistent admonition of Cuban meteorologists, who pioneered the art of hurricane prediction, leaders of the U.S. Bureau such as Willis Moore who led the National Weather Service in Washington; and William B. Stockman who was the forecast official for Havana, refused to give the warnings respectful consideration. Larson explains that Stockman "saw the people of Cuba and the Indies as a naïve, Aboriginal race in need of American stewardship." Neither man saw the necessity to sound the alarm. Those who so advised (Joseph Cline and Cuban meteorologists) were deemed too incompetent to be taken seriously. This boastful blunder on the part of Isaac and other officials resulted in the annihilation of 8,000 people; the literal extinguishing of bloodlines and the abortion of a city's potential.

OUR STATE OF EMERGENCY

This is why the book you are about to read is so important. It is my earnest attempt to "sound the alarm"—to say to America, particularly black America, that we are in a state of dire emergency. The African American race is indeed an endangered species. It is critical that we stop now and pay attention to the facts and contemplate their short and long term ramifications. The facts announce to us that a threatening race storm is swiftly headed our way. Presently, we are unprepared for its wrecking winds and staggering storm surge. For those who would doubt the legitimacy of this alarm, I dare you to FACE THE FACTS:

Physically: Blacks lead the way in heart disease, diabetes, fibroid tumors, infant mortality, prostate cancer, liver cancer, lung cancer, high blood pressure and other major sicknesses and disease. Black women account for 68% of new HIV/AIDS cases.

Academically: Only 56% of black students graduate high school by age 18. Only 20% of high school graduates who enter college can master college-level courses. A dismal 63% of black 4th graders cannot read on grade level and 61% of black 8th grade students cannot perform 8th grade math. On the SAT, black students score 220 points less than Asians, 200 points less than whites and 45 points less than Hispanics.

Financially/Economically: The average black family earns $30,000 per year, Hispanics $33,000, Whites $46,000, and Asians $55,000. Of the $688 billion blacks earn annually, we only spend 4% with African American businesses—96% of the wealth we earn is spent outside of our community. Per every 1,000 persons, Arabs start 108 businesses, Asians 96, Whites 64, Hispanics 19, and African Americans start only 9 according to *Solutions For Black American by* Jawanza Kunjufu.

Legally or Lawfully: One out of three black males is involved with the penal system. Black males comprise over 53% of the U.S. prison population. With a felony conviction, a person cannot vote, rent an apartment and they face many roadblocks in finding employment.

Family: Of black marriages, 66% end in divorce; and 43% of black families are headed by single mothers. Approximately 50% of black children live in poverty compared to less than 10% of white children.

You will be reading more disturbing facts, but you should review these figures again, slowly. Digesting each of them is important. Let me ask, if these trends continue to escalate and intensify: what does the future of the black race look like? Is our future bright or bleak? How long will we last—20, 30, 50 years? Who can be sure? Obviously at the rate we are traveling—in the wrong direction—we are headed for definite disaster.

Can you imagine an America with no viable African American community?

THE STORM IS INTENSIFYING

You need not be an expert in social science or a critical analyst of empirical data. If you are casually familiar with the facts previously stated, you know something is wrong—and if you are black and live in America, you know it intuitively. Even if you are a semi-conscious American, you are aware of the problem.

While blacks have, on one hand, made incredible strides over the past century, especially the latter half, it appears that our progress will be short-lived. There is a growing uneasiness due to intensifying pre-storm conditions. The wind is picking up and raindrops are steadily falling. Waves of consequence are quickly rising. This will not be a passing thunderstorm: something unusual and catastrophic is about to occur.

Despite the efforts of a faithful few who have sounded previous alarms, the masses continue business as usual. If these warning signals continue to go unheard and unheeded, it will prove fatal. This is yet another valiant effort to alert and awaken every thinking American, especially blacks, of our deteriorating predicament.

In view of these and other published statistics that paint such a gloomy picture of the African American plight, the question must be asked: *"Why are there not more trumpet blowers?"* *"Why isn't every preacher, politician, professor, corporate leader, and activist using every platform; employing microphones, cameras and pens to inform and incite action?"*

These issues will be dealt with in point blank fashion. You may or may not agree with what I have to say, but I do have an opinion—a strong one.

HOW WILL YOU RESPOND?

After you have read this book, you will no longer be able to plead ignorance. You will have heard the warning. At this moment, you are becoming knowledgeable and simultaneously responsible. Ultimately, you will be held accountable. The question you must answer is: How will I respond to the alarm? For starters, I suggest the following:

First: As you internalize the worsening condition, think of how you have contributed to the predicament in ways of commission and omission. Confess it and commit to discontinue destructive behavior.

Second: Look for people with whom to unite, who are dedicated to saving our community, whether they are African Americans or not. (There is much to be said on this subject in other chapters.)

Third: Empower those who empower us and reject those who do not empower us. Join people and organizations that are sensitive and serious concerning our plight.

Fourth: Make sure everyone in your concentric circle of contact knows you are reading this book and find a way to discuss its contents. All Americans, especially blacks, need to absorb more relevant and resourceful material. We waste so much time on foolishness. Our plight is so pressing that we cannot afford ignorance. It is unacceptable in this day of enlightenment for so many of us to remain in the dark concerning our predicament.

There is no time for majoring in minors while we minor in majors.

What's the latest fashion? That's minor. *How do we curve the drop out rates of black students?* That is major.

Who is ABC celebrity dating? That's minor. *How do we prevent the spread of sexually transmitted diseases among black teenagers?* That is major.

Where is the biggest party this weekend? What's the latest dance? That's minor. *How do we get a computer into the hands of every black student?* That is major.

How much did your last designer bag cost? Are your new wheels 18 or 22 inches? That's minor. *How do we open more black owned banks and other businesses in and outside the black community?* That is major.

Who is the latest celebrity athlete, entertainer or preacher? That's minor. *How do we revive proven family values in this pluralistic, post-modern society?* Now, that is major!

A PERPLEXING PARADOX

Every black church is at least aware of and more than likely has recited the phrase: ***God is good all the time and all the time God is good!***

Truer words have never been spoken. When our situation is examined, however, one must admit that these two propositions form a perplexing paradox. God is good all of the time, but blacks are doing bad—right now. Each assertion is undeniable. How can the two co-exist? This probing question must be answered: ***"If God Is So Good, Why Are Blacks Doing So Bad?"***

The answer awaits those who read this book.

CHAPTER ONE

A GENERATION DISCONNECTED

This is the first generation of blacks whose heroes are arrogantly illiterate, unashamedly immoral and irreverent.

S tamped forever into my memory are the feelings I had the first time I realized that a new breed of blacks had emerged. I was shocked, alarmed, angry and fearful. Most of all, I was concerned. I could see vividly, that unless something drastic occurred to address the situation, destruction was imminent.

The current crisis we face in black America today is the result of our failure to act courageously, comprehensively and most of all cohesively.

A SHOCKING FLICK!

The year was 1991. I was sitting in a movie theater in the "hood" viewing a film which had already sparked controversy. The news media questioned me outside before entering and let me know they would be awaiting my commentary following the showing.

Tension was thick as the sellout crowd of mostly young blacks stood in long lines and gathered on the premises. Police presence was increased—and I had brought along my own security for good measure.

The movie was *New Jack City*, starring Wesley Snipes as Nino

Brown, a violent, merciless drug kingpin who had taken over a neighborhood and would end up in a war against the police.

Because of my activism in the community, mostly on behalf of the issues of black people, I was invited to view the controversial flick to evaluate its content and potential impact on the culture. I had grown up watching black movies and had seen most of those released in the 70s, even some of which my parents would not have approved of; however, I managed to hook up with the boys to go and view them anyway. How we were able to get into some of those theaters, I don't know. But we did. So I had seen *Shaft, Superfly, Cornbread, Earl and Me, Coffee, Uptown Saturday Night,* and all the Bruce Lee movies.

Now here I was watching *New Jack City.* The violence was heinous. The sex was graphic. The drug dealing was an elevated profession and the gangsters were local heroes.

I remember well the scene late in the movie when the cataclysmic battle was raging between the thugs and police. I was shocked. The audience began chanting and cheering for the gangster thugs to win over the officers. This stunned me and caught me completely off guard, and I recall thinking to myself, "They really are pulling for the drug dealing criminals!"

I asked the staff members who were with me, "How did the drug dealers become the heroes, the protagonists in the story? When did wrong become right?"

DISTURBED AND DEPRESSED

Walking out of the theater, I was numb. Then I began paying closer attention to the demographics of the exiting audience. There were at least as many females as males—perhaps even more. The audience was mostly black with some Hispanics. The ages ranged from 15-35; only a handful were older.

I was 29 at the time, but had already been a pastor and community activist for 11 years. While I do not recall my exact statement to the press, I remember my mood. I was disturbed, disenchanted and depressed. I felt awkward because I realized there had arisen a new breed of black youth who were foreigners to me. One thing was certain: if I did not know and understand them, they surely did not know and understand me. I knew this was not a churched crowd and most likely not a schooled crowd—and would ultimately be a criminal and lost crowd. With their mindset, I knew they were destined to fail.

One thing I noticed was that a significant number of the audience who became angered by the crumbling of the drug ring and death of their hero were accompanied by small children. They were angry and hostile towards the law, order and the establishment. Their emotional outbursts were a proclamation of their resentment of anything which represented the system. I was sick inside.

It took me some time to process, analyze and reflect on the experience and begin to reach some conclusions. During this phase I asked myself and others with whom I dialogued, several pointed questions. I wondered, "Who are their parents and what sort of homes did they grow up in?" I questioned, "Had they ever been in church, to Sunday School, or did they know anything about the Lord?" I also thought, "What made them hate white people, particularly white cops?" And, "Why did they feel justified in disregarding the law, selling and using drugs? Why didn't the violence bother them?"

Finally, I wondered what were these mamas and daddies thinking bringing their children to an "R" rated movie that they knew would contain sex, drugs and violence—not to mention profuse profanity.

These were scary things to think about but it was necessary since these people really did exist and they looked a lot like me. This was my family, yet they were obviously disconnected from my reality and I from theirs.

WHAT HAPPENED TO VALUES?

My siblings and I, like many of our contemporaries, were probably in the last group to be trained in the values and principles that grounded and guided former generations of black Americans. I was raised in a Christian family, surrounded by people who were steeped in the values and principles of the Judeo-Christian faith. Early in life, I learned the Ten Commandments and could name all sixty-six books of the Bible by age 12.

Although I grew up in and around the hood and did my share of mischievous deeds, becoming a gangster or thug was not considered an option for me. While I was not at all sheltered, I was nurtured by a network of individuals and institutions which instilled the values of self respect, respect for others, respect for the law and respect for other people's property.

I cannot count the times I heard from my father, mother, grandparents, aunts, uncles and family friends, "If you lie, you will steal. If you steal, you will kill."

The penalty for lying in our house was next to execution! I will go to my grave remembering what the price was for not telling the truth.

I did steal a few plums and some sugar cane from neighborhood houses, but that was about the extent because I knew it meant the death penalty! Besides, I did not want God to punish me, nor did I want to go to jail. Most of all, I never wanted to break my parent's hearts.

WE WERE WATCHED

With these values, fears and priorities in my consciousness, I was not a candidate for street life. Although I fought the toughest, could hang with the roughest and could handle myself, I was respected. My parents were not about to raise a hoodlum in their house—and if you began looking, sounding or acting like one, you were immediately checked, in no uncertain terms. My parents and their supporting cast—consisting of close kin, church members, teachers and neighborhood mamas like Mrs. Emma Spikes—made sure we were properly indoctrinated, trained and watched. We grew up knowing what it meant to be black; what it meant to be law-abiding; what it meant to be Christian. This is why this *New Jack City* generation was so disturbing and foreign to me.

I knew there were bad and dishonest cops, but I still respected the law and law enforcement. I knew blacks had not been given equal opportunity to economic upward mobility, but selling drugs was illegal, inexcusable and destructive and therefore not an option. I was fully aware injustices still remained and that blacks had to stand up and fight for progress. But I also knew that violence was not the answer. I was raised on the Martin Luther King principles of love, respect and non-violence. His views agreed with those of Jesus and Jesus was, is, and will always be right.

WHAT HAPPENED TO MORAL ABSOLUTES?

There are countless experts who grapple with the complex issues related to this seemingly unreachable generation of black youth and young adults. Certainly a significant number are doing well, but it is without debate that many are exhibiting behavior not seen in any prior generation of blacks. There is a crowd on the scene today who do not fear taking a life; are not the least bit concerned with public perception; will say anything to anybody; will wear anything; do not mind going to jail and who have accepted violence as a way of life. Worst of all, they have no fear of God.

These are the children of the *New Jack City* era. They were raised by parents who took them to see movies that were "R" rated, blasted profane, vulgar and dehumanizing hip hop music in their ears from the time they were in cradles and infant car seats. These are the young adults who were raised on the filth aired on BET and MTV. They are the products of a culture that promulgates the idea that there are no moral absolutes. Consequently, they do not know when they are wrong. In fact, they are not sure what wrong *is!*

As best they can tell, wrong is wrong if it feels like it. Right is right only if it feels like it. But remember, they have been de-sensitized through the violent, sexually illicit, dehumanizing, God-dishonoring media by which they are indoctrinated.

THREE FUNERALS

I have heard too many stories that have convinced me this generation is, in many ways, disconnected. I have ministered at several funerals through the years where homicide was involved. Within a two month span of time in 2006 alone, I officiated three funerals of young African American men, each of whom had been shot by a young African American man.

One of these funerals was for "Big Hawk," John Edward Hawkins, an up and coming popular Houston rapper. He was slain in his driveway at point blank range by someone believed to have known him.

Another was shot in his driveway. The murderers stole the rims from his car. People close to him confirmed he was involved with drugs. The third was allegedly shot by his cousin as they argued over rims.

While the set of circumstances surrounding each of the slayings differs, there are some glaring commonalities. Each service was packed; Big Hawk's being the largest, quite naturally. Each of the crowds consisted of a multitude of self declared "THUGS FOR LIFE." This is a hip way of saying, "I'm Disconnected."

Neither of the victims were active in church and neither was in college or had a college degree. In each instance, a young black man had been forever silenced and, at the end of the day, the devil had won. *"The thief only comes to steal, kill and destroy."* His mission had obviously been accomplished.

WHAT GRIEF

I wish I had adequate words to describe the range of emotions a minister experiences in these situations. You grieve for the family. There sits a grandmother who doesn't understand what went wrong, but she is wise enough to discern the devil's work. A heart-broken mother for sure, is present; a father who has been there guiding and teaching...not likely. Siblings who know the culture of the day are there. Also present are some who are on the same path and others who are not surprised because they understand street life; but still they are all distraught.

Perhaps a young wife is present—stunned by the suddenness and permanence of her unimagined reality, with a look in her eyes that screams, "HELP." Worst of all are the children who are old enough to know what a funeral is and whose hero is in a casket being lowered into the freshly-tilled earth. There goes their provider, counselor, coach, role model, protector and disciplinarian—the only man whose presence gave them security, whose approval gave them confidence, whose touch gave them significance and whose embrace confirmed their immeasurable value. What grief! Then there is anger. The entire scene is so senseless.

BEYOND FALSE HOPE

Where is the love? If you could only convince this crowd of bewildered youthful mourners that you love them—really love them. If you could only convince them you care enough that you want to see them live the abundant life. Not what the world gives, but what our Heavenly Father offers. If you could only convince them you love them enough to want to show them a better way; one which is not false and doesn't promise quick, deceptive riches.

Because of your love, you tell them the truth. Although these are not words they want to hear, the truth is they are being deceived by the devil and by those he uses to lead them astray. He's got them chasing bling bling, Bentley's and Phantoms—those are the lures. Yet, in the final analysis, it's the path that leads to an early grave or to prison tours. *"There is a way that seems right but in the end, it leads to death."* Solomon, you were right!

A "THUG TIL I DIE"

Finally, there is the emptiness which comes when you have to admit that no matter how much you tried to reach them they may have listened or tolerated you only for the moment. But most are just dissing you! Some actually come forward to accept Christ after the funeral message. There are tears and looks of conviction etched on some of the hardest faces; sadly they don't make it back to church. The devil's enticement is too tempting and leaving their friends is too great a price to pay. They have made a commitment to being a "Thug Til I Die." How tragic!

Damn, I hate this. I hate the pronouncement, "Earth to earth, ashes to ashes, dust to dust." Thugs who are dealing don't grow old, spoil their grandchildren, retire and enjoy their golden years with the love of their lives. They don't build inspiring legacies to motivate and guide future generations. They don't leave the stage to earth's applause and respect, headed for heaven's ultimate award ceremony.

IGNORANCE OF THE PAST

The problem is black youth and young adults of this post-modern age are disconnected from their history, their heritage, their help and their hope. They are without any knowledge of who they actually are because they are ignorant of the past which has produced and shaped them. This holds true for too many blacks who are in leadership as well.

The extent of most black people's awareness of their history is a vague knowledge of slavery. We know we were at some point in time slaves in America. Most of our young people do not know when or why that was. They have no idea of who we were prior to leaving Africa. Many are clueless of the rich story of our evolution in this country and what it has taken to progress from slavery to holding positions as CEO's of fortune 500 companies, (albeit too few), governors, board chairpersons, NFL and NBA coaches, the world's best golfer, the nation's first black female billionaire, and so many more.

HOW DID WE GET HERE?

Knowing our legacy would lead our young to the conclusion that something before their arrival had worked. How else would you explain the enormous degree of black progress in a country that never intended for us to be a free and empowered people? Or how else would you explain our productive participation in a country which never planned for our inclusion and did not design space for our respected presence and whose laws were written considering blacks as property to be owned and leveraged? That is one reason why not knowing black history is so destructive.

Young black people have no idea what it actually took for them to have access to government services such as an education, due process under the law or the right to vote. How did we go from being called nigger, boy, gal, wench and heifer, in private and public, to being addressed as Mr. Chairman, Your Honor, Madam Chairlady, Mayor, Governor and Senator, not to mention being addressed as Mr. and Mrs. How did we make it from there to here? Something somebody was doing over a century ago, fifty years ago, before the 70s—worked!

THE HALL OF CHANGE

It certainly took more than a few heroic efforts performed by blacks who appear on the standard list whenever our history is discussed or celebrated. The list includes Frederick Douglas, Harriett Tubman, George Washington Carver, Mary McCloud Bethune and Jackie Robinson. These names head the Black American Hall of Fame and rightfully so. After all, it was Booker T. Washington who forged fresh educational paths for African Americans. It was W. E. B. Dubois who was an early exponent of full equality for African Americans, and who laid the groundwork for the National Association for the Advancement of Colored People. How could you not have Dorothy Height in the Hall of Fame when she significantly impacted every positive movement of African American women, in spite of physical challenges? When someone was needed as a spokesman in connection with the labor movement, A. Phillip Randolph accepted the challenge, knowing what the price would be.

Personally, I prefer to call these cultural icons members of the Hall of Change. That is what they were—Change Agents. They did not do what they did to become famous. They lived and died to bring about transformation.

PROGRESS BASED ON PRINCIPLES

Each, in his or her own way, helped to reshape American world history by creating a progressive chronicle that belongs to blacks in a unique way. But the progress blacks have made over the past 141 years, since the Emancipation Proclamation was signed, involved a countless cast of characters who lived, sacrificed and died for the cause. It was not done by a few who are frequently spotlighted.

The progress to which we refer is to be attributed to more than any conclusive list of personalities. Rather it is to be credited to the values, the vision and the principles that were once broadly embraced by blacks. This is the aspect of our history from which recent generations are disconnected, and unless there is a reconnection to these values, vision and principles, our race is forever doomed.

RECONNECTING TO OUR HISTORY

So, how do we rescue the race? Everybody wants to know the answer to this troubling question, but not all are prepared to hear it. We must figure out how to reconnect the coming generation to these basic values and beliefs that were once our foundation. To disconnect from our history is to disrespect the unheralded multitude whose blood and sweat watered the seeds of faith and belief that our day would be brighter than theirs. This is the first generation which doesn't seem to care.

This is what I heard in Bill Cosby's speech at the NAACP Gala, celebrating the 50th anniversary of Brown vs. Board of Education, the landmark case determining segregation of public schools to be unconstitutional. It is also what I heard as he continued to speak in the town hall gatherings across the country. It is a theme repeated by many preachers whose voices are not amplified beyond the walls of their sanctuaries and whose faces are not broadcast into the homes of millions by television satellites. It is what I hear every day when speaking to burned-out, frustrated teachers who remember when students were different—when they paid attention in class, sat down when they were told to do so and were terrified when their parents were called about misbehavior.

This is what grandparents who are fifty, sixty and seventy are saying when they speak about the crisis of fearing their own offspring and not knowing how to relate to children of their own bloodline. I hear the same story when speaking with parents who have no control over the children they feed, clothe and house. Haven't you heard these conversations?

At work, at church, in barber shops and salons, it's always the talk: "What in the world is wrong with these people?" This is the frequently asked question. The experts are not the only ones who comprehend the disgusting predicament. The masses, everyday people, are keenly aware that something is amiss.

Blacks know things have gone wrong and have not turned out the way we envisioned—so many of us are unemployed and unemployable. So many locked up in prison and poverty and locked out of prosperity. We feel the reality our economic weakness causes on a daily basis and sense the absence of leadership that is bold and visionary. Even blacks who are not statistically informed are experientially aware of our perishing predicament. We see the unraveling of the thread that once held us together.

A COMMON CONNECTION

Most blacks are in agreement with Cosby and others who argue the point. So is this author. We are talking about the values, beliefs and principles that were once our common connections. This is what guided and guarded us from external adversity and oppression as well as from self-destructive attitudes and behavior.

The heroes and heroines we list in the Hall of Change definitely inspired us. But be assured, their mission would not have been successful if their values-based messages had not resonated with their generation. Our challenge today is that our values do not connect us. We no longer believe the same things.

"THOU SHALL NOT KILL!"

Several years ago, I started a community based organization for youth called Good Gang USA. This was an innovative response to the escalating violence in our neighborhood due to an increase in gang activity. Almost nightly, there were reports of youth involved in criminal behavior. I actually got an idea from a friend, Pastor John Raphael of New Hope Baptist Church in New Orleans, who, for the same reason, had posted signs around the city that read, *"Thou Shall Not Kill!"*

After several murders in our area, mostly due to crack cocaine, we took to the streets and also posted signs proclaiming this message on trees and utility poles. We literally saturated our area with the signs painted in red.

THE ROCK SLINGERS

I received a call late one night, actually before daybreak, that a murder had taken place. I arrived at the crime scene to discover a young black male, 19 years old, had been shot to death. Above his head on a telephone poll was posted one of our signs, *"Thou Shall Not Kill."*

Afterwards, I spent time with his younger brother, 17, who witnessed the murder. I was amazed at what I learned in our conversation. The bewildered and grief-stricken teenager confirmed that it was drug related, as suspected. The street corner had been known for some time to be a hot spot for purchasing drugs, especially crack cocaine. Making a buy was as simple as pulling up to the stop sign, money in hand, and the rock slingers would boldly approach your window and process your order. It was as easy as using the drive thru lane at McDonald's and just as public, too.

I marveled at how the dealers could remain open for business for so long in the black community. Selling drugs in plain sight would never be accepted or tolerated in Houston's River Oaks community where the richest citizens live. Why can it happen in Acres Homes? We have to wonder.

NO SENSE OF RIGHT OR WRONG

In this incident, a white male in his 30's came into the hood to score some crack from the boys. When he ran out of money, he agreed to rent them his car for a few days in exchange for drugs. The problem was, after he sobered up, he demanded his car back prior to the time agreed. The boys evidently would not relinquish the vehicle willingly. When the man managed to take back the keys and was fleeing in his car, the teenager threw a brick and broke out a window. Then, with a rifle, he fired one shot, killing the youth instantly.

A horrid story, for sure, but what shocked me equally was that the younger brother could not understand how he and his brother were at least partially responsible because they were peddling drugs.

In his troubled mind, the only criminal was the murderer because he broke the contract with the car deal. Selling drugs was only illegal in the youth's mind, not wrong. This mindset caught me completely off guard. He had no concept of right versus wrong.

"What do I say to him?" I pondered. He had no fundamental belief to which I could refer. There was no war raging within him, not the kind that burns within me. Paul, the noted evangelist in scripture also confirms this to be his plight. *"When I would do good, evil is always present,"* he said. On yet another occasion Paul admits, *"There is a war within me."* He acknowledged there is an ongoing feud between the flesh and the spirit, right and wrong.

THE FOUNDATION OF BELIEF

Like this kid, there are so many young brothers and sisters on the scene today who are either ignorant of or do not embrace basic Judeo-Christian values. Historically, through the scriptures, we were taught and learned a view of God, of others, of self and the world that dictated how we related, responded and reacted to all of the above—love, respect, compassion.

To say African Americans have been a religious and deeply spiritual people is a gross understatement. Actually, we have always understood the reality of God, His faithfulness to us, and our dependence on Him. How else were we going to overcome the cruel systems of evil that tormented and traumatized us? How else were we going to escape the traps designed to restrict and prohibit our upward mobility in this country? And how else would we be able to survive the dehumanizing tactics of biological, psychological, emotional and economic warfare? We have always trusted God to be our deliverer.

Blacks have always known it would take God in His mercy, might and miracles to deliver us from the tyrannical powers that were imposed and enforced in America's unequal system of justice, and from the opportunities for self and group success. But we also understood the only way God would help us is that we would have to be right. Therefore, for generations, we instilled the values gleaned from scripture into the cultural consciousness of the group.

By so doing, we knew He would fight with and for us, and He did.

GROUNDED SOLDIERS

There could never have been a Booker T. Washington, or W.E.B. Dubois without these values. There never could have been a Fannie Lou Hammer or Rosa Parks without these beliefs. There would not have been a Medgar and Myrlie Evers or Martin and Coretta King were it not for the values and lofty ideals taught in the sacred text.

Moreover, there would not have been the anonymous yet enormous supporting cast of characters who contributed to the movement by praying, marching and embracing non-violence as a true expression of loving the enemy who despitefully uses and abuses you. The supporting cast of soldiers was grounded in the same values as were the leaders. This is why they were able to commit to the cause. They spoke the same language; therefore, they could advance a common agenda. They were motivated by identical principles and were passionate about their collective pursuits.

THE BLING-BLING GENERATION

In the history of blacks, we discover what makes us a distinguished and rich people. We also discover what makes us strong and resilient. Not knowing or being disconnected from our history is so costly for young African Americans for several reasons. First, it leaves us bankrupt of the values and beliefs that have secured us in periods of uncertainty and stabilized us when we had no standing in the world. Second, it gave us an unshakable sense of self while we were considered chattel and treated indignantly and inhumanely.

Antipodal to former generations, this group is seeking to be distinguished by being brash and rude, by cash, not character; diamonds, not dignity; materials, not morals. This is the warp in today's value system.

"It's all about the Benjamins" ($100 bills) is their attitude, and bling-bling is the external evidence that you are a baller and shot caller. They do not understand the value of internal richness—that who you are is more important than what you have. This is why there are no limits to what they will do for money and external trappings.

A Spiritual Passion

This is opposite of how our ancestors, upon whom our positive history is constructed, previously thought. Earlier blacks were driven by a different "ethos" and exhibited a different "pathos." They were determined to always be distinguished by their morality, spirituality and intellect. There was a time, in fact, when whites would defer to the God of their Negro servants, maids and nannies. They perceived Negroes had a different kind of relationship with God than they themselves knew. Our extreme spiritual passion has always been a cultural distinction.

Even while oppressed, blacks were conspicuously devout and circumspect and generally more committed to treating their neighbors right than one would expect under the circumstances. This ethic even made its way into a standard Negro hymn, "I will Trust In The Lord." The lyrics in one of the verses say: "I am going to treat everybody right...til I die." The other verses all deal with one's dependence on God. But this one phrase addresses how one should treat his neighbor. This was a basic motif in former black culture. "Everybody" meant everybody including those who were the antagonizers of the Negro.

Desperate Dependence

For years, many whites and some blacks have struggled to make sense of the extreme passion displayed in the cultural distinction of black worship. This is in contrast to the majority white experience that is obviously more cerebral, stoic and staid. This one dimensional form of expression makes for a more personal and internalized experience (although this is changing). Blacks on the other hand, have a multi-dimensional recipe for an encounter with God. We act out to God our inner convictions and we fully display our delight and utter dependence on Him for blessings and help with burdens. He has always been our help. Historically, we have acknowledged, embraced and extolled God as our Savior from the tyranny of sin and as our Deliverer from the control of a satanic system that only He could help us overcome.

This topic cannot be exhausted here, but allow me to offer some insight. One of the motivating sources of black's extreme exertion in praying, singing and preaching has been our immense, enduring and exclusive hope in God. I call this concept "desperate dependence." That is, African Americans have always been aware of the fact that the severity of our plight required the intervention of the "Divine Being" who loved us and is unequivocally able to defend and deliver us. A people group whose common plight has never required this kind of Divine assistance will always find it difficult to recognize or grasp this concept.

We have been ever aware of our disfavorable and disadvantaged position in America, and when we have suffered momentary amnesia, something would happen to snap us back to reality—like the assassination of a freedom fighter, or the lynching of James Byrd, Jr., a black man in an East Texas town in 1998. Something like the beating of Rodney King, being stopped by police because you are black and driving through the wrong neighborhood, even when you live there (racial profiling); or the atrocities exposed by Hurricane Katrina such as poorly constructed levees and inadequate response of federal agencies on behalf of poor people, mostly black.

It has always surprised others how blacks could remain so positive towards God in the midst of the kind of struggles we have endured in this country. Thinking about this, one of my white friends who is a millionaire made this comment. "Watching your church members praise God with all their hearts was amazing and convicting," he commented after visiting one of our Sunday services. "We [whites] who control so much wealth go to church and fall asleep. But blacks, with all they have gone through and still tolerate in America, praise God so joyously. Man, God has to have a special place in heaven for black people," he concluded.

ALL THINGS WERE POSSIBLE

This reputation of being distinguishingly spiritual has survived the ages. It was this culture-wide understanding that God is good—no matter how bad life and people are—which generated our exuberant expression towards Him. And, of course, as long as this view dominated our culture's thinking, blacks made progressive leaps that only divine power could have caused. Without Him, we could do nothing, was our historical understanding; but with Him, we believed all things were possible.

For too many new-generation blacks, God has become an afterthought, which has caused a collective digression of passionate spirituality. We have a drastically different collective view of God than our forbearers did, causing a reduction in our reverence for Him, rebellion against sacred rules and resentment towards those who remind us of our wrong way. We are far less spiritual than were our forbearers who depended on God for everything—from guidance to protection, from justice to daily bread. Out of this dependence for every article of clothing and morsel of food grew unparalleled devotion that was respected within and without black culture. Everybody went to church!

THE POST-MODERN PSYCHE

Not only are we less spiritual than ever, we are also flagrantly less moral. The collective cultural consciousness of blacks with regards to right and wrong has sharply eroded. The line which divides the two has faded to an almost invisible gray. Lifestyles that were not long ago unthinkable, unfathomable and unacceptable in the black community have become commonplace and "in your face." Overt disrespect, disregard and even disdain for the laws intended to govern morality all attest to our generation's disconnection from the conveyors of our history and heritage. Historically, we have always been fearful of God on some level. Even the wayward and disobedient were acknowledgers of the path that is right when it was clearly understood.

Far too many in this generation are either ignorant or simply

31

dismiss the timeless laws as antiquated and irrelevant. In the post-modern psyche, there is virtually no acceptance of the fact there actually are Divine Laws which are immutable and irrefutable. There is no room for this kind of Supreme right to governance in the new ideology. This results in overt disrespect, disregard and disdain for persons who assert and attempt to enforce rules based in a Righteous Mind. Lifestyles that were not long ago unthinkable, unfathomable and unacceptable in the black community have become commonplace and "in your face." This is not only true in black culture, it is also a scopious reality among white and Hispanic youth and young adults. It is a trademark of this age to be anti-authority and adverse to any promulgated absolutes.

Divine absolutes are resented and vehemently rejected by the post-modern psyche, thus the code of ethics commonly embraced by this culture is at best situational. This means, wrong could be right and right could be wrong if the situation regards it. This is how many in our day rationalize and justify corrupt and violent behavior. They deduce that their actions are appropriate based on the situation they find themselves in.

The spirit of post-modernity evaluates man to become his own sovereign. As such, he inherits the right to be unrestricted, unrestrained, and unaccountable to no one except himself. This is why so many people who have been raised in this era are incapable of submitting to any imposed standards or any form of authority.

If one embraces this concept of Divine absolutes and theology, it would follow that it would be reflected in their anthropology and sociology. There would be a view of man that demands respect, love and benevolence. It would also require a personal code of conduct which supports the well being of society at large. Criminal and unethical behavior would be deemed abnormal and unacceptable. But because the spirit of post-modernity seeks to elevate man to the level of the Supreme Being of his universe and ultimate authority, he is incapable of submitting to laws beyond those he self imposes or prefers.

NO FEAR OF PUNISHMENT?

I grew up afraid of God, which was not uncommon among my contemporaries, neither was it uncommon to blacks raised before the seventies. Black families once instilled in each new generation the reality of the Sacred Laws and the awareness of an ever present, all knowing God who punished the transgressors. (Admittedly, too little emphasis was placed on repentance.) Today, there is little thought of the consequences of living contrary to Divine Law. Dark passions are often practiced in open light.

Obviously, dark passions are nothing new, but the fact they are widely accepted as normal behavior is different. More alarming is this generation's audacity to defend immoral choices and lifestyles. This is the *Desperate Housewives* and the *Drop It Like It's Hot* era. Lewdness, profane erotica and heinous violence dominate the artistic expressions of this new generation. They major in the undoing of the previously embraced beliefs and boundaries.

TALKING TRASH

It has been said that profanity is the tool of weak people attempting to sound strong. More than any former generation, this crowd has been responsible for popularizing profanity. Obscene language dominates casual conversation, movies scripts and music lyrics. Today's content is rife with vulgarity. Every other word is B _ _ _ h this, MF, suck this, lick that... There was a time when this kind of talk was considered filth, garbage and trash. When our parents heard we had used a "bad word," it meant a whipping, or at least washing your mouth out with soap.

The two dialects mastered by this generation are "sewer" and "street." Language of the street is the official vocabulary of the hip hop generation. Some of it is actually cool, but in most instances it is taken to a disastrous extreme. It is intended to connect those who are in defiance of conforming to the mainstream and are the unabashed values that formerly shaped black culture's ideological, philosophical and sociological constructs. Street language is identifiable by phrases such as "What up dawg?" "Dats my nigga." "Fitty" (fifty) and "fo" (four).

33

Effort is consistently made not to sound proper, educated and like you have been shaped by mainstream Americanism. Speaking English accurately is viewed as being white versus right, which equates being black with ignorance. Self declared "Thugs For Life" are only committed to knowing and using street and sewer vocabulary, which sentences them to the same. They should be mindful that they are in America, which is larger than the small space they occupy in their reduced interpretation of black America.

DWINDLING OPPORTUNITIES — VERBAL VICTIMS

Those who protest the use of proper English and are content to mastering sewer and street vocabulary become victims of their own verbiage. They place themselves at a verbal disadvantage and can only know a pseudo sense of power. Real power is accessed through infiltrating and matriculating in established institutions such as education, government, corporate America and the finance industry. Neither sewer nor street language works in any of these arenas. Adults who subscribe to these limited dialects are incapable of representing themselves or their children when necessary. They are unable to communicate with teachers, prospective employers, potential clients and their elected representatives. How do you apply for a bank loan if you cannot communicate with the banker? This is why the "Thug For Life" mentality disempowers this generation. It is also why other races are taking advantage of opportunities that blacks are ill-prepared for. Real power will never be accessed by a "dumbed-down" generation.

What you hear and speak will directly influence how you think and behave. The content of one's ongoing conversation will determine one's concepts, character and conduct.

PARENTAL DYSFUNCTIONALITY

Unfortunately, the worse thing that has ever happened to some children are the mothers and fathers they are stuck with to raise them. The dysfunctionality of parents is a major reason blacks are doing so bad. There is a dearth of credible, principled and responsible parents in our community. Some of the examples I have witnessed have angered and sickened me to the point of a turned stomach. In many instances, youth are tolerated who are knowingly participating in illicit and illegal activity. How does a parent come to celebrate their children's illegitimate pharmaceutical entrepreneurship (drug dealing)? How does a parent stoop to the level of accepting dirty money as hush money using it to pay bills and support lavish purchases? This is all too common in black and other minority communities. Parents who fit this profile should go to jail with their kids when they are caught! Knowingly housing, feeding and supporting a criminal is the work of an accomplice. They are ruining a kid and wrecking a community.

Then there are parents who allow their children to participate in illicit and immoral behavior. In fact, it is encouraged in the way they allow girls to dress, dance, and date, unscrutinized and unsupervised. When a parent allows a 12-year old girl to wear a thong (sexually suggestive underwear), pants cut below the navel, short skirts that advertise "I'm hot," they are co-promoting their daughter as a sex object. It should be no surprise that so many young girls are sexually active before their 13th birthday. The fact that only a few boys are raised with any moral foundation and are left to randomly conduct misguided masculine exploits is, too, a fault of today's parents. Too many of our sons have no concept of respect for the opposite sex and the obligation that comes with making babies—thus the "Baby Momma" syndrome.

Where are parents while all of this self-destructive, race-debilitating behavior is taking place? The excuses are unlimited, but none are sufficient. This problem must be corrected. Parents must accept the responsibility of knowing and caring about where their children are, who they are with, what they are doing and what the associated consequences are.

Finally dysfunctional parents are those who fail their children by not being a worthy role model. Parents, the best example your children should see of dignity, integrity, human decency and moral fiber is you. Tragically what many mothers and fathers say and do

35

in front of their children is evidence of their disconnection. Even worse are some of the things parents do with and to their children. Parenting is a 24/7 commitment and those who neglect their responsibility will not leave a rich legacy nor enjoy their children's respect.

FORFEITING MORAL AUTHORITY

In many instances, youth are tolerated who knowingly are committing immoral and illegal acts. I remember being sexually curious and exploratory, but it was all kept out of sight and at a minimum. There was much more talk among the boys than there was action. But, good Lord, the way these girls dress in thongs, low cut pants far below the naval, and skirts that advertise "I'm Hot," is more than suggestive. In many situations, they are celebrated at home for their gangster images, illegitimate pharmaceutical entrepreneurship and prowess in the streets.

Parents with the moral conviction passed on by our forbearers would not tolerate such behavior. They would demand change or file charges themselves. Again, this is not a matter of money; it is a matter of morals.

DON'T CALL ME – (TOUGH LOVE)

I recall hearing my grandfather, the late Rev. C. D. Dixon, say, "If you go to jail for stealing, selling drugs or killing somebody, don't call me to come and get you. I am not going to waste my money on such foolishness. I did not raise you to be a criminal or a thug."

Not only was this his position, it was the philosophy of most black parents a few decades ago. They did not play games when it came to being law abiding and morally upright. These were the parents who knew your friends, your friend's mama and daddy and would tell you who could and could not call and visit their house. There were certain individuals you could not be seen with because your parents had discerned them to be bad company, which meant their moral makeup was flawed. This was value-based parenting and it produced generations of positive, productive and principled families. Ultimately, these were generations God could bless and use to promote our race. We owe decades of progress to that version of the black family.

The problem is, today's young people are being raised by too many unstable, weak parents who lack the fortitude to administer tough love. Consequently, they spoil undisciplined, rude and unproductive kids. This too must be corrected.

WHAT IS THE MARK?

I am not suggesting at all that former generations were pure and without blemish. Certainly, sin has had its expression in every person of every generation, including this author and his family. Mischievousness among adolescents has always been common, and I have my share of stories which links me to fallen humanity. There is, however, a difference in missing the mark and not aiming for the mark at all!

Even worse is the fact that in this new generation, so many don't even know what the mark is! How can you possibly hit a target when you do not know what or where it is located? The sad reality is that another generation of blacks has been raised in large part by people who have never been shown the goal or given the standard. The unparalleled violence, unrestricted erotica and unbridled vulgarity are all manifestations of a lawless and decadent generation who are not directed by an internal moral compass. They are unable to identify the way that is right.

THE DEBASING OF WOMEN

There is a preponderance of evidence that this generation of blacks is not connected to our legacy or traditions—and consequently they are behaving in ways that are uncharacteristic of our culture. The degree of disrespect shown for children, elders and of course our women, is a symptom that cannot be ignored. This has rarely been a part of black culture.

The things we do to our women, the names we call them, the way we treat them in private and in the public eye are often horrible and repulsive. This is not what it means to be black. Slapping women on the butt, grinding them in public or in a music video, and beating them, is not an authentic black expression.

I applaud the young sisters at Spellman who refused to accept being portrayed in rap music as sluts, freaks and mindless sex objects whose goals in life are to simply satisfy the animalistic and sadistic desires of self described pimps and bosses.

It is our heritage, our tradition, to treat women with the utmost respect and to demand that others, including our children (especially) sons do the same. Dogs do dogs in public. Men should never be seen reducing themselves and women to the level of animals in heat.

Sisters (black women) need to be taught and led to revolt against the desecrating treatment to which too many have grown accustomed to receiving and accepting. The debased image of black women on TV screens, in videos and sung about in music is designed to reduce women to mindless subjects, fit only to be slaves and objects of pleasure to their mad, mentally and emotionally disturbed masters.

We must teach African American girls not to answer to misogynistic mislabels and not support those who degrade and denigrate them in exchange for money.

In black heritage there were unwritten but well-communicated rules, one of which was: a man is not supposed to hit a woman—ever. Were there men who did so? Yes! Were there consequences? Absolutely!

Men who were known to physically abuse women in the black community were criticized and ostracized. They were deemed cowards—and worse. One of the most offensive crimes a boy could commit was to hit his sister or a girl in the neighborhood. Your daddy would convince you very quickly that this was unacceptable.

The stronger specimen taking advantage of the weaker vessel was an act which brought embarrassment and shame. Men who abused and fought women were viewed as less than a man. That is why we can clearly see how disconnected this generation is from black heritage.So many brothers are abusive of our women: beating, demeaning, slapping, even raping them. Any man who feels "macho" after hurting a woman is deranged and troubled by demons.

I heard Minister Louis Farrakhan present a major piece on this demonic practice some time ago. On this we agree: God is judging black men because we neglect, disrespect and fail to protect our women. Traditionally, black men were educated and raised to nurture, support and protect them. Once again, we must raise up a generation of African American males who are taught to "Treat Her Like a Lady."

IGNORING THE TRUTH-TELLERS

In the days of Dr. Martin Luther King, Jr., black Americans served the Lord, the children were in Sunday School, and most Negroes attended church and sought to obey God. For they had seen and understood how God had worked miracles on their behalf by delivering them through changing oppressive laws that had been used to keep them down.

In absence of the values, traditions and beliefs of black heritage which once shaped our culture, there is no longer ground for embarrassment or shame. This is why this new generation can commit the most heinous crimes, do the most insidious and disgusting things, participate in the most filthy conduct and never feel the need to apologize, repent or change. The consequences of our disconnection from the people, principles and practices of what once empowered us continue to prove deadly.

A void of God-centered leadership was created when Dr. King and his generation of God-fearing change agents died. A new generation of blacks arose who did not know the Lord, neither were they made to understand all that God had done for African Americans. Even when they were told, they ignored the truth tellers and would not learn their peoples' history which declared God to be their helper.

39

The Saga of Disobedience

The sons and daughters of former black God-fearing servants became evil in the sight of the Lord and addicted to idol gods—such as money, earthly materials and bling-bling. They declared "It's all about me, cars, clothes and cosmetics." They turned their backs on the God who had proven trustworthy to their grandparents, for He had delivered them from slavery, brought them out of Jim Crow and segregation. Now a growing number of them were moving out of the hood to the burbs, shopping in malls, driving new cars and catching planes. They began to serve the idol gods worshiped by other people who they were now allowed to hang out with. They stopped praying and worshiping and stayed home on Sundays, washing their new cars, hanging on the corner, chilling and getting high. All this ticked God off!

They dissed their Maker, gave their souls to the devil and fell under the spell of idolatry, resulting in all kinds of wicked behavior. They turned their neighborhoods into dope infested territories that were controlled by foreign forces who demanded them to get more and more of their own relatives hooked on brain-frying, life-destroying chemicals. This turned their streets into war zones and bloodshed became the rule. They boldly declared themselves to be "Thugs for Life," "Hoochies, Hos and Pimps." They became wild and wicked in their sexual expressions. Perverted sex became the norm; homosexuality and lesbianism ran rampant and even churches would not tell them differently, because they were motivated by profits, not prophets. Their politics were also polluted.

Then God became violently angry with them. Although He loved their souls, He allowed those who hated, despised and oppressed them to take advantage. They became the leading revenue generators for the prison industrial complex and the biggest profit producers for the hidden faces who really controlled the entertainment industry, who exploited them by paying them to degrade their race, abuse their women, poison their children and curse God to His face.

Wherever you found these people, they were in trouble. In schools, they performed below average and led the dropout rate. In business, they struggled with few corporations and controlled little to no wealth. In health, they were the sickest, as cancer, AIDS, hypertension, diabetes, Lupus, heart disease and strokes plagued them in disproportionate numbers. They became a byword and a laughing stock as other races who were weaker, who once respected their race, surpassed them in every significant category. The Lord had promised them progress and prosperity as long as they obeyed, followed and worshiped Him. But He also promised destruction and calamity if ever they forsook Him.

Now that the hand of the Lord was against them and things were obviously out of control, they were miserable and distressed. They knew they had offended God and called out for mercy and help. Then because He really loved them, God raised up some new leaders who would tell the truth and lead these people to destined victories!

RESCUING OUR FUTURE

The above is a 21st century paraphrase of Judges, Chapter 2: verses 7-16, with cultural application. I believe it to be of utmost importance for blacks to hear and understand this message. The truth is, blacks owe all of our progress in this country to the favor and power of God and to former generations who believed, trusted, obeyed and served Him. They did so unashamedly. He is, and always has been, our help in ages past and our hope in years to come.

God of our weary years, God of our silent tears;
Thou who has brought us thus far on the way.
Thou who has by thy might, led us into the light;
Keep us forever in thy path, we pray.

Lest our feet stray from the places
our God where we met Thee;
Lest our hearts, drunk with the wine of the world
we forget Thee.

41

Shadowed beneath thy hand, may we forever stand,
true to our God. True to our native land.

How did we make it from there to here? Through our history, our heritage, our hope and our help. If we reconnect, we can rescue our future. If we don't, we are definitely doomed.

CHAPTER TWO

INTELLECTUAL EROSION

EDGE-U-CATION is the passport to prosperity.

If a person disagrees with my argument that blacks in America are doing poorly, as some have attempted to do, I simply challenge them to examine the facts with regard to our current state of intellectual erosion. There is a preponderance of evidence that we are missing the boat educationally.

I marvel when I read and re-read the writings of men such as W.E.B. DuBois and others who, despite circumstantial adversities germane to their times, advanced in their academic pursuits. Although fresh out of slavery, they managed so quickly to gain an edge over their former masters and the elite thinkers of the day, through their relentless quest for knowledge. How they were able to gain such a firm grasp on a varied scope of disciplines and master the skill and art of communication, is still a wonder. Even more, it should be an eternal source of inspiration to every black boy and girl to seek intellectual development. When mental prowess is laid on a solid spiritual foundation, it becomes the power to change the world for good.

THE WINNING EDGE

Trying to make authentic progress in such a competitive and cruel world with an untrained mind is equivalent to cutting tall timber in a thick forest with a dull axe! Consequently, major structures are never built.

As a result, I have devised a new way of spelling "education" which hopefully makes the point much clearer. The new spelling is EDGE-U-CATION. Why? Because an education gives you a winning edge.

The fact only 46% of black students graduate by age 18 is alarming. The statistic that 63% of black 4th graders read below grade level is shocking. These and other facts reveal why we have lost our winning edge.

A major problem across the country has to do with drop outs. The rate for blacks and Hispanics is more than astounding. In my state, Texas, the Intercultural Development Research Association reports that 2.5 million students dropped out of school in the past 20 years. 69.3% of these were blacks.

START EARLY!

Most black students who graduate from high school and enter college are not prepared to take true college level courses. To think you can be successful in America and be illiterate is an insane proposition. We must dispel the myths by which many of our youth have been deceived.

One contributing factor is the "slow start" a majority of African American children have on their academic journey as reported by the Intercultural Development Research Association. Just 45% of black children enroll in early childhood education by age 3, and by age 4, only 73% are registered. These stats are also published in the book, The Covenant, by Edmund W. Gordon. With these facts in view, it is unthinkable that anyone should propose cutting funding to programs such as Head Start. We must do more to help parents understand the importance of an early childhood education.

ACADEMICS OR ATHLETICS?

It is my conviction this requires a shift in mentality.

Recently our family was blessed with the birth of a son, James III. He weighed 9 lbs. 5 oz. at birth, a hefty baby for sure. Instantly, the talk about him being a fullback or linebacker rather than a scholar, engineer or commercial real estate developer could be heard. Why? Because a part of our culturally inbred psyche is to hope for, look forward to, some even pray for star athletes to come from their loins. Black parents peek with excitement at any sign which suggests their boys may have celebrity sports potential. Sadly, we often fail to look for, notice or expect academic scholarship.

This perception is one cause of the educational achievement gap between blacks and students of other races—which has not diminished in the past decade. Unfortunately, athletics come second or third to education. Reading, math and science comes first!

Another explanation for blacks lagging behind is that students around the world and in the U.S. are spending more time studying and applying themselves academically than are African American kids. Asians lead, whites are second, Hispanics are third and African Americans are last. Rev. Jesse Jackson makes the point repeatedly that black students spend more hours than other races participating in sports, talking on the phone and watching television. Of course, black kids out-perform others in areas outside the classroom and predominantly black school sports teams win championships—but fail to win awards for academic achievement.

Still another reason for the wide gap is the large number of African American youth who have bought into popular myths that are deceitful traps. One myth being you can rap and dance your way to success, making an education unnecessary. They see gold, diamonds, luxury rides and mansions that are mostly rented for a video shoot and begin to imagine themselves living in such opulence. They unwittingly decide this is an easy path to fame and fortune. Mindless of how deceitful glitter and glamour can be, gullible youth become disinterested in the classroom. For them, rap and starring in videos, as many young girls aspire to do, becomes the vehicle to prosperity. But there are testimonies to the contrary.

A HIGH PRICE TO PAY

In her book, *Confessions of a Video Vixen,* Karrine Steffans reveals the seldom told truth about the real life of this grossly immoral, illiterate and irreverent culture.

Karrine, a sharp, smart woman, tells of being raped, beaten, drugged out, emotionally, mentally and sexually abused, and eventually penniless. Sure there was glamour, money, fame and men—lots of them. But at the end of the day, she came to her God-given senses and realized it was the devil's trap.

Unfortunately, she did not change until she was BROKE and BROKEN—a high price to pay for choosing a path painted pretty by the devil which only leads to desperation, dysfunction and destruction. "There is a way that seems right, but the destination is death," a very wise man named Solomon once said.

THIS MYTH OF "PIMPIN'"

Another myth has to do with the matter of "pimpin.'" This is the new generation's idea of being a strong, successful black man. You may ask, "Are you serious?"

Pimpin' has become a widely accepted way of life and career in 21st century black America. How is it a term which was viewed with concrete disdain has become the bold declaration of a young culture—the passionate ambition of the males upon whose shoulders the future of black America rests? This is jacked up any way you look!

How do the sons of Frederick Douglass and Booker T. Washington resort to pimpin'? How do the sons of Charles Drew and Medgar Evers choose pimpin' as the way to express their creativity and ingenuity? How do the sons of Malcolm and Martin stoop to pimpin as their contribution to the race—if there is such a thing?

Our fore parents must be turning over in their graves. We will be known as the generation that took pimpin' mainstream. Now we even have TV shows with titles such as "Pimp My Ride" and "Pimp Out Your Crib."

To comprehend how disgraceful and irreverent this concept is, one must understand what the term means. Being a pimp has to do with managing weak, distressed and desperate women who sell their bodies for money and give him all the cash. In return, the pimp provides for their basic needs and protection. It's a relationship based on degradation and manipulation. In other words, pimps demoralize women and use them to support their flamboyant lifestyles. Any version of this twisted mentality is sadistic and pathetic.

EQUAL OPPORTUNITY?

Still another reason black students lag behind is the disparity in school quality. In the words of Edmund W. Gordon, as he writes in The Covenant, we are still, "...a society where opportunities to learn are unequally distributed." This means all schools are not equitably funded and supported. In fact, Gordon goes on to assert, "Schools that serve predominantly black student populations are more likely to be under-resourced than are schools serving predominantly white student populations. Students attending schools in predominantly white neighborhoods are less likely to experience teachers of poor quality than are students attending schools in predominantly black communities."

As the writer of Ecclesiastes says, "Money answers all things." Everybody knows you get what you pay for. So how is it we expect schools in black neighborhoods to perform and produce at the same levels on less money? You cannot duplicate the same house for $250,000 as can be built for $500,000. Therefore, parents, churches and community leaders should pay much closer attention to school funding issues. In this and other ways, schools in the hood are often set up to fail.

"WHATEVER IT TAKES"

Across the U.S., predominantly black schools that once were landmark institutions and symbols of pride and power are in trouble. Many are on life support systems, struggling to stay alive. This is true in Houston, Texas, where I live, and where such an example is Jack Yates High School. Named for one of the most influential blacks in our city's history, this school has graduated some of the most impressive personalities our nation has known: famed jazz musical genius Joe Sample; Emmy Award Winner and two-time Tony Award nominee, dancer and actress, Debbie Allen; Gerald Smith of Smith Graham Company, an investment banking firm with offices in Houston, San Francisco, New York and London. These are the tip of the iceberg. They all graduated from Yates Senior High School before integration. And, while there have been some impressive alumni since that time, the school has greatly declined.

Today, the school's reputation is not what it was. Yates High, instead of being heralded for academic excellence, is now known for academic under-achievement. Although when I spoke at a recent program to their graduates, I was greatly impressed by some of the students. Unfortunately, top achievers are in the minority and the negatives make the news.

What is more than ironic is that the school is named for Rev. Jack Henry Yates, a former slave who according to documented history, learned to read at the tutelage of his owner's son. Following the Emancipation Proclamation, he continued his education, eventually becoming an educator, entrepreneur, activist and a minister. He founded many churches—including the one I pastor today. His "whatever it takes" example strips students in the 21st century of any excuses.

WHERE ARE THE PARENTS?

A serious problem we face is that too many parents are not engaged in their children's education. I founded Dominion Academy Charter School for 6th through 8th grades, specializing in business, economics and entrepreneurship; and I know first hand the problems that result from disengaged parents.

Why is it schools have such a challenge motivating parents to attend important meetings? Why are so few members of Parent Teacher's Organizations? Why do mothers and fathers attend athletic games but never show up for Open House?

The point is, a parent is inept who is not passionately involved in their child's school career. The message of apathy this sends to government and corporate America is not a positive one.

Government must be held accountable for doing the right thing toward predominantly black schools, but by whom? Corporate

48

America should be expected to invest in inner city schools, but by whom? When parents disengage, others unplug. This is the problem.

NO MORE WASTED MINDS

Parents, preachers, teachers, elected leaders, civic servants and entertainers must all begin to aggressively declare and instill in the minds of our youth the idea of empowerment through academic elevation. We cannot afford to produce another generation of anti-intellectuals who become parents themselves. We must do everything we can to make practical and personal the motto of the UNCF....*"A Mind is a Terrible Thing to Waste."* It must be affirmed again and again to every child, "YOUR MIND IS TOO VALUABLE TO WASTE." And we must hold every responsible party accountable for their role in the process.

Dropping out of the education race is a sign of giving up on attaining the prize our fore-parents passionately believed to be within our reach. I literally cringe when I hear young sisters and brothers express, "This is the white man's world. It ain't going to ever change, no matter what we do."

No! This is God's world and while we live and breathe we have a right to be all we can be. We should have the courage to prepare ourselves and improve everyday. Our ceiling becomes the next generation's floor.

We shall overcome,—if we continue overcoming!

CHAPTER THREE

WE WORK LESS AND WANT MORE

Being slothful, lazy, shiftless and unproductive is not a reflection of authentic blackness. Those who portray these images misrepresent our culture and hijack our legacy.

One significant attribute in our heritage that is grossly absent in this generation is WORK!

The black race is doing badly partially because too many of us have lost our zeal to work. A large contingency in this generation abhors labor and, in fact, disrespects brothers and sisters who work hard—legitimately.

The problem is they have not been *raised* to work. First, they lack discipline. Second, they have no skills. This crowd believes in reward without sacrifice and are wallowing in self pity. Being raised on handouts has had an adverse effect on the psyche. It softens the will and erodes a sense of personal responsibility.

There are absolutely too many of Booker T. Washington's sons walking the streets during the day and night, carrying cell phones, wearing sagging pants, smoking blunts, looking bad and acting important with no job and no look of expectation in their eyes. There are too many of Sojourner Truth's daughters lying around with men to extract money for bills, walking around with fatherless children, indoctrinated with welfare mentalities, with no dreams of greatness in their spirits.

This is not germane to our history or our heritage, and it is distorting and damaging our legacy. In times past, blacks have been a most ambitious and an impressively industrious people. Working our way up in the world has been a cultural characteristic for generations.

KEEPING IT REAL!

Even in times of extreme adversity, bigotry and oppression, we maintained a commitment to working our way through. Men, women and children all worked—and holding multiple jobs was not uncommon. Blacks were once known and respected by their peers and other races for their work ethic—just as other ethnic groups are today. For example, it is not uncommon to hear conversations among blacks admiring and applauding Hispanics and Asian brothers and sisters for their willingness to work, their abilities to toil together, and the quality of their efforts. Every black person I know has had this conversation. (We are keeping it real).

Why are these no longer the conversations held about blacks? Unless and until they are, we will become more and more a burden to each other and to society. If you have relatives who are adverse to working, you understand the point I am making.

When was the last time you walked into a corner store, a gas station, a dry cleaners or a restaurant, that was owned and operated by a black family? Do you know a black owned landscaping business where the kids work with their parents? These were not rare sites in years past. Have you passed by a construction site lately? How many blacks did you see working? How many blacks do you know who are carpenters, brick masons, plumbers, concrete pourers, or roofers? These are jobs blacks once filled, but today they are mostly held by Hispanics. They are raising families, sending their children to school and buying homes on these jobs. Neither of these examples describe black families most of the time. When was the last time you read a story like this in the pages of Ebony—not to mention seeing it firsthand?

A disproportionate number of this generation of new school African Americans are not the working kind. Some are overwhelmed with a spirit of defeat. Others are convinced that the world is too unfair and are possessed by a spirit of discouragement. Still more are simply content with cheating, scheming, begging and gold digging. Then it gets worse, because there is the group of misguided and maladjusted youth who are robbing, stealing and in general—thuggin' and drug dealing. They call it hustling. The law calls it crime. Sociologists call it violence. The Bible calls it wickedness. We need to get the message across to our youth and young adults that you cannot build a legitimate life on an illegitimate premise.

Unfortunately, too many of our youth buy into the misguided thinking that views work as slavery, especially when it requires working in someone else's business. They use this mis-definition of work as justification for not getting or keeping a job, declaring that they will never slave (work) for someone else.

Even many who have entrepreneurial aspirations often make this mistake in judgment. They do not realize that the greater percentage of today's business owners formally worked for other people.

Am I suggesting that blacks and other minorities should be satisfied doing outside manual, blue collar labor? Of course, I'm not. The point I am making is all work that is legal and moral is also noble. A person who earns $40,000 per year pouring concrete is more honorable than someone who sells drugs and makes $500,000. I am also saying that if you desire a $300,000 white collar income, then get a $300,000 per year education. Do not drop out or get a G.E.D. and expect that kind of career.

What these uninspired individuals need is to have a conversation with a black living legend, someone over 65, who actually picked cotton in a Southern cotton field. They need to go on a tour of some of the most prestigious landmarks in America and the world to see what their ancestors built with no hopes of a paycheck. Most of these young African Americans don't have a clue.

This is why I do not get emotionally entangled with excuses which are too frequently used to cover up laziness, unpreparedness and a lack of zeal.

Remember, this is the generation that wants tennis shoes that cost $100, designer jeans, bling bling on their fingers, around their necks and in their mouths; they want 22- inch wheels that spin, and expensive rides. They want so much, to work so little. Those who think like this are set up to fail.

WHATEVER IT TOOK

"Where there is a will, there is a way." This was the mind set that motivated former generations to overcome obstacles, endure injustices and prove to be invincible against the odds.

When my grandfather, C.D. Dixon, went to work on Sunday, he was our pastor. But when he went to work on Monday, he was a janitor at Heights State Bank. We were equally proud of him on both days.

When I was a kid, my dad's primary job was a funeral director and mortician (the consummate professional) at Carl Barnes Funeral Home. This establishment was founded by my mother's grandfather in 1932 and was later owned by her father, Titus Barnes. But during a period of financial distress in our immediate family, my dad took an evening job at CLECO, a manufacturer of oil field drilling equipment. He wore suits and dress shoes by day, and khakis and work boots by night. He was never embarrassed and we were never ashamed of him. Taking care of his family was his priority, and he did it legitimately. He worked. I recently found a golf ball bearing CLECO's logo. It brought tears to my eyes.

Now that I think about it, all the men intimately connected to me and my family during childhood worked, which rubbed off on me. My brother Tim and I, along with my cousins mowed grass during the summer. We worked at the funeral home at night and on weekends. We painted, sacked groceries, and took other odd jobs. The bottom line is—we were industrious!

One summer our neighbor, Mr. Thomas Miles, hired us on along with his son, comedian and actor Thomas Miles II, to help construct metal storage buildings. It was blisteringly hot and the metal would cut your hands if not held properly. But it was great and I learned to drive a truck with a standard transmission that year.

Now, my father and Thomas Miles, Sr., both work for me. I am blessed.

Our parents and grandparents taught, "Work always comes before play!" I heard that statement a thousand times—and "If you do not work, you will steal; if you steal, you will kill," two thousand times. The Bible even says in 2 Thessalonians 3:19, *"...if anyone is not willing to work, he is not to eat either."*

SISTERS, THIS IS INSANE!

Believe it or not, there was a time in the black community when people, especially men, who would not work were not respected. A man who refused to get and keep a job could not attract a decent woman. We need to return to this way of thinking. Nowadays, our young sisters will go to school, acquire an education, get a job, buy a house, buy a car and then hook up with a brother who has no education, no job, who claims he is hustling, drives her car, sleeps in her bed, and enjoys the *candy* and the refrigerator. He is a player and a pimp, at her expense. Sisters, this is insane! If a brother cannot pay (legally), don't let him play and do not let him stay!

What's shocking is how many black women there are today who will tolerate men who will not work. Believe it or not—this is real! However, real men desire to shoulder their own load and to be providers for their families. We want to be heroes by providing and protecting our women and children.

"WILLING WORKERS MARCHES"

On another note, has our government failed us by not protecting our citizens who are willing to work from profit-motivated abandonment by American based corporations? Yes! Has the black working class and others been betrayed and shafted after being faithful to building companies and industries into the multi-billion dollar empires they have become on American blood, sweat and tears? Yes! Should this be addressed? Absolutely!

Dr. Kwanza Kunjufu estimates that 3,000,000 middle class insurance-paying jobs have been lost in America due to this betrayal by business. Add to this the trauma caused by the technological revolution which found millions of unskilled black workers unprepared and the results are devastating. There was no plan to retrain our work force to fit them for 21st century

I propose that all over America there needs to be "Willing Workers Campaigns" and town hall meetings to get the attention of policy makers. *"I will work, create a job for me!"* Why isn't there a program to attract new jobs to America's inner cities. This question has to be asked.

If this isn't effective, we need to stop buying products of those who send all their middle class manufacturing, benefits-providing jobs overseas. Companies and the government should be required to invest in the technological education of students in every city and community. Every kid needs a computer!

There should also be a public outcry for greater emphasis and commitment by the government to fund job training programs. All of this is null and void however, if African American parents do not recommit to training children in solid work ethics. We have to take every opportunity to give our kids responsibility that challenges them to use their minds and their muscles to be productive.

By the time I was 17, I had been a window cleaner, mowed lawns, washed cars, been a bus boy, sacked and stocked groceries, sold vacuum cleaners and been a shoe salesman. Although I became a pastor at 18, I found time to drive a delivery truck and shine and repair shoes to supplement my meager income (from the church). I thank God for the work ethics that were modeled for me and which molded me. I'm still a hard working black man and proud of it.

It is time to reclaim our heritage of honest, character-building work. Parents, teach your sons the voice of work. Someone's daughter will thank you. Teach your daughters to work. They may need to take care of themselves and eventually contribute to the household income to make ends meet. Remember, a people who will not or cannot work become unnecessary in a capitalistic society. In fact, they become a liability.

CHAPTER FOUR

WE ARE ALL FLASH, NO CASH!

We have an intoxicating infatuation with swiftly depreciating consumer goods. We work to buy, not to build; to spend, not to save; to impress, not to invest. Consequently, we are on the bottom rung of the economic ladder.

Have you ever wondered why the majority of blacks "out dress" and "out drive" our white counterparts—even the people we work for?"

To say "we over do it" is an understatement. Actually, when it comes to matters of the exterior, we *grossly* over do it, but regarding internal matters we do the opposite. We spend the most on things which are valued the least. So much of our hard earned income is spent on cars, clothes, cosmetics and accoutrements which are cute and eye catching, but lack any real lasting value beyond appearance. More than any other race, this is our proclivity—and the results are devastating. With each new generation, we raise a fresh group of conspicuous consumers who inherit our *"All Flash and No Cash"* mentality.

What Happened?

Why is it that the ethnic group responsible for countless inventions upon which the American economy is based earns less than others who have contributed less? How is it the people upon whose ancestral backs rests the foundation of America's unrivaled global economy are the most economically disenfranchised group in the nation? Why has the race most responsible for changing the course of American history ended up being the ones taking least advantage of laws it helped to change and opportunities it helped to create?

For example, if blacks had not made segregation an issue, Brown versus the Board of Education would not exist—which opened doors to public education for all minorities. The Civil Rights Bill of 1965 would not have been signed into law. And what about affirmative action which paved the way for economic and educational opportunities? Obviously, neither of these landmark decisions would have occurred without the leadership, determination and sacrificial work of blacks. So how and why is it we remain on the bottom rung of the economic and educational strata? And what can be done to significantly improve our condition in the 21st century? These are troubling questions that beg a response.

A Return to Begging

We are not the enslaved group who populated Egypt. Neither are we wilderness residents. Actually, we are the first wave of Promised Land inhabitants and are the inaugural occupants of the land of awesome opportunity and increased possibility. But like our forerunners in history (biblical), we have not handled our prosperity well.

This is why I am sounding the alarm. On the surface we appear to be true possessors of the Promised Land, however, when the hard facts are faced, we must admit that we are not solidly situated. In fact, unless drastic changes are made, we are on our way back to a begging and demeaning state.

To the credit of the civil rights era, its leaders and freedom fighters who were vigilant about our liberation, the shackles of segregation were broken and the doors to education and economic opportunity were forced open. For the first time in American history, blacks could prove their capacity to matriculate alongside others and vie for jobs. It is inspiring to think of how a people so long held back and blocked out could quickly compete and contribute. The brilliance and genius of blacks are undeniable facts of history. Positions we filled, strides we made and the value we added to the American economy swiftly changed our economic reality. We obtained jobs where we formerly could not, opened businesses, launched ventures and comprehensively moved up in the world.

While it is true that the mid-20th century advances have created the largest "Black Middle Class" in our history and helped to produce an Oprah Winfrey, Robert Johnson, several thriving corporations and a few Fortune 500 CEO's, collectively blacks are doing poorly.

AN ALARMING GAP

The difference between the median income of whites versus blacks is $16,000 annually. However, the per capita wealth between the two is $45,000. The size of this gap reveals alarming differences in our spending patterns. Blacks as a whole are more consumer-oriented than are whites. We reflect the unwise servant in scripture who was unfaithful with the least.

This is a behavior in our culture which must change if we are to ever realize our dream of being an empowered and self-reliant people. It is a fault in cultural character that has to be called out and dealt with by leaders at every level. It is one of the primary reasons we are lagging behind. This "Flash without Cash" mentality undermines every possibility of building stable families, strong communities, viable organizations and enduring institutions. It is why black America, sadly, is not a power, but a prey. This mentality is adverse to creating patterns of generational wealth, acquiring appreciating assets and controlling a market share of any significance. Without any of these, it is impossible to gain respect or be considered resourceful in a capitalistic environment.

Should these trends continue, tragedy awaits. One of my friends, Anthony Wilcots, reminded me of the wisdom shared with him by a former mentor. "Everything in America is about money," the seasoned minister told him. This may sound a bit too unspiritual, especially since the gentleman was a minister. But another wise man, long, long ago, made a similar statement more emphatically. *"Wine makes merry and a feast brings great laughter, but money answers all things."* His name was King Solomon.

VISUAL EXCESS

Blacks must soon learn that it is cash, not flash, which equals true wealth and real power in our communities, our nation and the world. If one observes the way we dress, drive, drink and decorate ourselves, you would think our income and per capita wealth far exceeds other races. You would conclude we are prosperous.

Attend the average black church this Sunday and you'll see the excess. The parking lot will be filled with the latest models of luxury vehicles, many sporting wheels that were custom ordered to jazz up the ride. The BMW's, Jaguars, Lexus, Mercedes Benz, all sorts of SUV's abound. Very few cars will be four years old and paid for. We are slaves to monthly payments with interest on depreciating items; a problem we will address in this chapter.

EXTERNAL EXTRAVAGANCE

Stand at the door of a black church and you may forget you are in church at all! You could be attending an Ebony fashion show featuring the top designers of the day and models of all shapes and sizes. There is no shortage of Gucci, Louis Vuitton, Chanel, St. John and Bruno Magli. From eyeglasses to jewelry, suits to dresses, footwear to underwear, there are name brands that all demand great price.

A look at the pulpit will probably reveal a visual message which speaks as loud (maybe louder) and perhaps clearer than the sermon that is to come. A great number of black pastors have mastered the art of external extravagance, even more than they have mastered biblical exposition and relevant truth telling. It is not always obvious there has been sufficient hours in focused study and preparation deliver an insightful and impacting message. What is perceptible, however, is that they have spent time meticulously coordinating their wardrobe as everything is sure to match and shine. From Armani to Versace, from Zanetti to Ferragamo and Santoni, from Rolex to Bulgari—it's all there. Messages advocating high morality, devotion to missions and ministry are often overshadowed by the gaudy display of materialism.

Unfortunately, in too many instances, the preacher's wardrobe is more organized than his thoughts. If you could check his house, more attention has probably been given to his closet than his study. It seems some preachers are caught up in a competition to win the apparel award.

Some high-profile ministers may be in a different "cash class" and have earned the right to wear custom-tailored suits. Don't feel you need to copy them. Preachers at all levels need to understand that the goal should not be to impress the hurting, needy and struggling people being spoken to, but to enable them. While I do agree that the messenger of empowerment should be a model of the principles being proclaimed, unbridled extravagance is a distraction.

IT DOESN'T ADD UP

This pricey pattern of fashion parading is certainly not limited to the black church. It is a community-wide phenomenon. Check out the nightclub scene, attend a banquet or black social function and it is the same thing. You see it repeated at a Congressional Black Caucus weekend or a National Baptist Convention. The evidence is obvious: we will spend money on clothes and accessories if we do nothing else. We actually plan our travels around shopping; often it is how we measure the worthiness of a trip to a particular place based on the shopping venues. Malls are magnets to our culture of materialism. We are the fashion queens and kings of America. We win—the trophy is ours, but we are collectively broke! It really does not add up. We even promote the idiotic saying, "Shop 'til you drop!"

Where it Really Counts

It happens at every level. Follow our children to school and there they are, the fashion princes and princesses among other students. Often richer white kids are wearing Levi, Wranglers and Keds. They shop at Old Navy or Wal-Mart. Our children, on the other hand, are wearing Sean Jean and Nike. This is a generational epidemic that is destroying us. We have dropped in our economic standing, and will continue spiraling downward if present trends are not reversed. We spend so much money and expend so much effort to be impressive in all the wrong places.

The message black leadership must begin to get across to our race, and especially into the psyche of our young people, is: "It counts at the bank, not on your back!" Winning compliments at school, the streets, the clubs, at church, work or at a social function means little if you command no respect at the bank.

We are impressive people in every place except the financial institutions. We take pride in our wardrobe wizardry, color coordination and apparel acumen, but we are losers at the savings and loan offices. This is where the table turns.

At financial institutions, no one is impressed by the price of the suit, shoes or jewelry; the balance in your account is the only thing that matters. Being fashionable is given its true and proper value—zero! You see, at the bank, the façade quickly fades. Why? Because we fit the description of high-risk customers. We have minimum cash and are maxed out in credit. We owe everybody and nobody owes us. We are always the borrower, not the lender. When we complete a loan application, the accounts payable column is loaded and the accounts receivable column is empty. Making matters worse, the items we are paying for on credit are often without value. We may be applauded and complimented in so many other places but at the bank we are the least powerful or respected.

As a race, we do not need classes, lessons or seminars on how to dress—rather, on how to invest. Instead of coaching on how to acquire an extravagant wardrobe, we need to understand how to build wealth. Often in black circles, there are jokes made concerning the lack of fashion sense in other races. But I can only imagine the reciprocal humor whispered by others about flamboyant-dressing, black people driving luxury cars who are dead broke.

It's not a laughing matter!

ARTIFICIAL LOYALTY

Many of us are desperate for acceptance. We are constantly trying to work our way into new groups and into the hearts of other people—especially if they have (or appear to have) more material goods and status. This can prove dangerous. While it is not necessarily a bad thing to want to break into new circles, there is need for caution. First, people who demand that you spend money to keep up with them are not genuine. Therefore, they will never be true friends or partners. They are phony and will not be loyal. Remember this: *"Bought loyalty is always artificial and too expensive."*

You never want to be accepted on the basis of your dress or status symbols. This is not who you are, so never reduce yourself to this level. Also, do not allow anyone to impress you to the point that you will become a slave for acceptance.

COMPULSIVE ADDICTIONS

The black community's chronic need for approval, applause and acceptance makes us easy targets for advertisers and retailers. We are suckers for a sale! We are a huge market that advertisers take for granted. We are impulsive buyers with a compulsive addiction to status symbols because this is what makes us feel important. By the way, when have you heard advertisements on a black radio station promoting estate planning, a business seminar or how to retire wealthy? Check out the billboards in our communities versus white communities. The messages are drastically different. We are encouraged to buy liquor, clothes, cars, and other depreciating commodities. Things that sparkle, but have no lasting value.

Black people need to think! We must comprehend the psychological strategies that are designed to keep us economically disempowered. We need to understand why the "All Flash and No Cash" mentality is so pervasive in our community and why each new generation is bound to repeat the same insanity, unless we change.

FEELINGS OF INFERIORITY

Best selling author, Dr. Michael Eric Dyson, in his book *"Is Bill Cosby Right?"* does a brilliant job explaining the history of blacks and our bent towards flamboyance in fashion. He attributes much of the behavior to the determination of black elitists attempting to distinguish themselves from lower class blacks, while at the same time find acceptance by upper class whites. Of course, blacks of lesser means counter by doing whatever is necessary to be accepted and not be upstaged by the black middle and upper classes.

Even deeper, I believe this behavior is revelatory of a major flaw, the root of which is a severe inferiority complex. This is not a mere accusation; it is an admission. While it is not a popular thing to say, it is nonetheless true. The value we place on external image far exceeds the thinking of someone who possesses a healthy self-worth. This inferiority complex runs throughout our race, from the elitist few to middle class and to the poor in the hood. *"Blacks are concerned about image to the point of paranoia,"* says author, Juan Williams. The fact is, blacks suffer with several debilitating diseases: materialism, greed, an extreme inferiority complex and a pervasive sense of inadequacy. This compounded condition is the hidden basis underneath the chronic consumerism that we practice. It fuels the "All Flash and No Cash" syndrome.

Not only does our unaffordable extravagance reveal an inferiority complex, it also exposes a level of greed and materialism that undermines our quest towards authentic prosperity. We love "stuff," crave things and are gripped by insatiable appetites for whatever makes us feel better about ourselves. Things that make us feel equal to or better than other people. We dress, drive and decorate ourselves to evoke compliments and applause from others. Plus, we are hooked on the fleeting feeling of superiority generated by new and expensive things. This is deceptive because spending money you don't have will soon produce symptoms such as depression and anxiety. It can also contribute to health issues like hypertension, stress and heart problems.

WANTS VERSUS NEEDS

The saying is true: *"We spend all the money we have on things we don't need, buying things we can't afford to impress people we don't like."*

We shell out cash for $200 weaves, carry $300 cell phones, sport $500 grills (not on the front of a car, but in the mouth) yet at the same time we have no health or life insurance. What...a savings bond? Not to mention a parcel of real estate or any other legitimate investments such as stocks and bonds in our portfolio. In other words, we sacrifice, bend over backwards to impress others, while failing to take care of ourselves and the people we love. We are more committed to wants than we are needs—which places us in great jeopardy. This is even true in what we *pray* for.

Sadly, many go to school and take a job just to satisfy these *wants*—a Jamaican vacation or a luxury watch.

It's time for a change!

NO SATISFACTION!

My high school economics teacher, John Harper, drilled a principle into our teenage minds and spirits I personally will never forget. *"A want is never completely satisfied."* He preached this everyday for an entire semester. Over the years, I have learned from experience how truly profound the statement is. The message is simply this: You cannot ever spend enough or have enough to cease wanting. Wants are *always* wanting!

You purchase a new car today and for a month, it is all the car you will ever want. Three months later, you're paying attention to another make and model. You buy a new dress and it makes you feel like you're the sharpest thing around, but this too is short-lived. Soon you decide you want something new to create the same heady feeling which came with the previous outfit.

No matter what the category, wants are never completely and permanently satisfied. This is why blacks must learn to accurately distinguish the difference between wants and needs.

Wants are bottomless holes. Needs, however, have definite boundaries and are not open-ended:

- You need transportation. You want a new Mercedes.
- You need a house. You want the biggest one on the block.
- You need decent clothes. You want designer labels.
- You need to eat. You want steak and lobster.
- You need water. You want an $8 cocktail.

THE PRICE OF PLEASURE

What Mr. Harper endeavored to teach his students is that if you commit to, live to, or work to satisfy all your wants, you will always be broke. In other words, if you are a slave to your wants, lack will be an undesirable but permanent companion. This explains why there are so many sisters with too many luxury shoes and purses to count, yet they can't pay their utility bills. And why so many brothers are wearing $500 suits with no savings accounts. It also is the reason so many parents look like they have it all together, but cannot afford college tuition for their designer-dressed children —and why so many in church dress, drive and dine nicely, yet when they die, family friends and the church have to pay funeral expenses.

In far too many instances, our principles are twisted and foolish practices follow. We are more passionate regarding pleasure than we are priorities. This comes at a great price because pleasure is deceptive. A wise pastor in our city, Dr. A. L. Patterson, opened my eyes to this principle. *"Any pleasure experienced through our five senses is not capable of satisfying beyond a two hour period."* He explains this is because all such pleasures diminish with the use of them. Meaning, as you eat, wear, drink, or otherwise experience these things, the pleasure they bring is already dissipating. Whatever you ate two hours ago is providing no pleasure now; no matter how good it tasted. Whoever you slept with last night is providing no pleasure today. Whatever song you heard this morning is providing no pleasure this very minute. As soon as the experience is over, the pleasure it produced quickly subsides.

This is the deception of any delight discerned through the senses or emotions. Anyone who does not have mastery over their passion for pleasure will pursue it recklessly. They will always over- do it— over-spend, over-drink, over-dress, over-sex—and the list goes on. Anything over done becomes a vice, which grips and is hard to shake. It is why all pleasure must be kept in moderation.

A Reality Check

The "All Flash and No Cash" predicament is one with which we have become dangerously comfortable. It is also risky. Those who make it a habit to exist this way are like skaters on thin ice with the sun shining. You can only skate for so long before the ice gives way. Do not allow the momentary sense of security to deceive you. This is where black America is today. We have been seduced into this dangerous and risky mode of existence—having mastered looking like what we are not. We operate on the faulty principle *"Fake it 'til you make it."* The problem is, faking it often undermines any chance of *really* making it. Because the imitation has a price tag and is often too expensive. Understand this, *"Ain't Nothing Like the Real Thing."*

Keeping it real, really works because truth will prevail. Here is why. The people you attract while faking it will eventually find you out. A front can only be maintained for so long. I am not advocating going around with a sign on your forehead which reads "I am broke." The point is, just don't get caught up in trying to maintain a façade that drains the blood out of you. You need to be wise and use discretion. Learn how to dress to impress without going overboard. And whatever you do, don't start believing you are there before you arrive! Keep your reality in check. Your bank statement will speak more truth than your clothes closet.

Maintaining a façade your budget cannot support will cause you to compromise values and leads to devious behavior. Too many of us have learned how to manipulate the system to acquire depreciating items required to keep up our fronts. We become masters at falsifying documents, lying to creditors, creating bogus identities and using multiple addresses, all to maintain a fictitious image that wins temporary applause and artificial acceptance. There are women who know well the "buy it this evening, wear it tonight, and return it tomorrow game." This is done to appear classy at an event, but only a "class-less" person would stoop this low. This and other such dishonest behaviors will never be blessed by God.

BORROWERS, NOT LENDERS

On the surface, to look at us one would think we are a genuinely prosperous race, but the truth is 50% of our children live in poverty. People find it hard to believe that our black colleges are closing due to lack of support and our per capita wealth is less than all other major ethnic groups. We appear to be owners, when we are employees. We have the image of investors while we are mere consumers. We are borrowers rather than lenders.

My friend, Drayton McClane, owns the Houston Astros baseball team. Frequently, he invites me to join him as his personal guest at Minute Maid Park, which is a different way to view a game. On one such occasion, I left my office going straight to the stadium without having time to change into my usual ballpark attire; khakis and a golf shirt or slacks and a sports jacket with no tie. While sitting next to the billionaire team owner, I began to take inventory of the scene.

I looked over at Drayton and I thought to myself. "He is worth a billion. I am worth—well, not a billion. Yet! He is attending the game for business; I am here on pleasure. I am counting strikes, outs and runs. He is counting fans, hot dogs, beverages and memorabilia sold. I feel good sitting in a coveted seat behind home plate. He owns all of the 40,950 seats in the arena. Tomorrow, I will brag about where I was, while he will go the bank with a considerable deposit. I will take an autographed baseball or T-shirt home to my children. He's building a trust fund to give to his descendants later. He is wearing a pair of simple slacks, a shirt and tie from a department store and shoes that could be worn everyday. I am wearing an Italian made suit, a custom made shirt with French cuffs bearing my initials, a high priced tie and a pair of expensive gators. "Drayton was *Cash*; I was *Flash*." To look at us, I appeared to be the owner and Drayton the guest. The thought embarrassed me.

I am also ashamed as an African-American when I consider our "all show and no go" reality. We should all feel this way since we did not inherit this backwards way of thinking from the best in our ancestral legacy. Our leading ancestors understood that to become an empowered race would require economic independence. Even an elementary education in black history will reveal how industrious and progressive blacks in former generations thought.

SHORT-TERM GRATIFICATION

It is a given that as a people, blacks started out behind—about 300 years behind. But despite all of our work, it is taking us too long to catch up. With seemingly no conscious or concern for consequences, we max out our cash and credit on things which depreciate, showing total disregard for the future. We spend today like tomorrow will never come. It is our habit to over-commit to immediate, short-term gratification. The vast majority of blacks are caught up in this vicious cycle of poor stewardship, thus we are in a self-destructive mode. What outside forces are not able to do to destroy us, we do to ourselves.

There are too few messages being delivered on this subject. How many black leaders and celebrities are advocates of this truth? Where are the black publications that include this message in their content? When was the last time you heard a black celebrity promoting wise budgeting? Even in our primary venue of communication and education, the church, there is not nearly enough said and done to address this crisis. Hats off to the ministers and community based leaders who do so. The problem is there is a dearth of those who teach and stress financial literacy and legitimate economic empowerment. All of our churches, however, place major emphasis on giving. There must be a call for balanced teaching on financial discipline. People cannot give what they do not have, and often they do not have because of ignorance and lack of self-control. There is much damage taking place due to a deficiency of knowledge. Churches that do not teach a balanced approach to financial stewardship actually perpetuate the problem. Again, those who are the exceptions should be highlighted, complimented, and most of all emulated.

MISSING SKILLS

Some clergy seem to focus more on what they can get from people than what they can give to them. All too often the plan for prosperity only includes the pastor. This is tragic and sickening —and unbiblical.

Regrettably, too many are not attending the kind of churches that have their comprehensive best interest in mind. On the other hand, there are many pastors who are concerned, but lack the capacity for adequately addressing the issue because they don't have a grasp of the problem.

Unfortunately, few black finance professionals are connected with church ministries, especially those in the inner cities where the need is most severe. The black middle class detachment from urban centers continues to take its toll.

In all fairness, many churches are too traditionally structured for forward thinking middle class professionals to plug into their system. They only offer choirs, deacons, ushers and other traditional ministries to participate in. These are certainly necessary, but there has to be relevant opportunities created to attract the technical gifts and skills of those who can bless (enhance) others through their exposure and expertise. The lack of financially astute persons as a part of the church's teaching apparatus is crippling. The other difficulty is convincing people to have confidence in those who are sincerely trying to teach them to live responsibly.

Sadly, some tend to believe more in church leaders who abuse and misuse them because they promote quick fix strategies that don't work. Building financial stability and success never happens overnight. It requires long-term commitment to a process that is painful before it is gainful. The result of our collective ignorance and lack of discipline is a persisting pattern of over spending on things which don't last and are of little value.

A Disturbing Contrast

There is certainly no lack of flash among our celebrities and superstars. Back during the glory days of the Houston Oilers (Warren Moon's era) and the Houston Rockets (Hakeem Olajawon's era), I served as chaplain and chapel service leader for both teams. The Oilers came close to going to the Super Bowl and the Rockets won two NBA Championships, back to back, during my tenure with the teams.

It was amazing to observe what a vast difference there was in one player's mentality from another. While in uniform, they were all professional superstars doing brilliant things which evoked worship from millions who saw them as god-like beings. But out of uniform, off the field or court, there were obvious differences in mentality, which showed in how they handled money.

During that time I noticed an interesting and disturbing trend. Off the field the black players wore the most expensive clothes and jewelry and drove the most expensive cars. This was true, almost without exception. Only a few practiced moderation. Even the rookies got immediately into the parade upon signing contracts. Many of them were known for driving several vehicles worth more than $100,000. On the other hand, the white players were generally more modest. Although they too made millions, they were out-dressed and out-driven by the brothers.

Check it out for yourself. When a black professional athlete is being interviewed after a game, standing on the sidelines or benched due to injuries, most of them look like they're not at a ball game, but modeling for GQ. Brothers know how to style! In direct contrast, the white players will be in jeans, tennis shoes or boots. They seem completely oblivious of the need to impress other players, fans, or the TV audience with their attire. For that matter, they are equally disinterested in attracting attention on the streets with their one-of-a-kind flashy chariots. Brothers are more likely to have pimped out rides that can hardly go unnoticed. This is the image black youth have of African American athletes who are more influential than teachers, preachers and, unfortunately, parents.

REDUCED TO POVERTY

I also noticed how frequently the white athletes spoke of buying and investing in real estate. This is not to suggest there were no blacks who did the same. But a disproportionate number did not practice the kind of moderation and financial prudence as their white colleagues. To their credit, I know of several brothers who did invest and continue to prosper after the conclusion of their professional sports careers. However, the sad reality remains, so many did the opposite—choosing to squander their pot of gold on depreciating items. They threw the biggest, most elaborate parties, drove the flashiest cars (several at a time), bought the most expensive toys, sported the finest wardrobes, wore the largest diamonds (on the fingers and in the ears), supported all the leeches—and a few years after their careers had ended, had so little to show for all the time and hard work it took to reach the pros.

It is sad to see former black athletes working common hourly jobs after making millions. This is true of entertainers as well. I'm sure you can think of several who were once on top of the world, making crazy money. For a short run they lived like kings and queens but because of their gross mismanagement of resources they have returned to poverty.

I also know of preachers who fit this description. They were leading pastors and popular pulpiteers who preached to full houses all over the country. Many pastored churches for three to five decades and during their careers they drove Cadillacs and Mercedes Benz. They were sharp dressers who made fashion statements when they stood before crowds who revered them. But at the end of their ministry when it was time to retire, they could not because of inadequate financial preparation. They became burdens to the people they formally blessed. Upon the death of many pastors their widows and families are left to the mercy of their congregations. I've seen former first ladies (the title given to the pastor's wife) who once walked with dignity, end up working as clerks or cashiers in department stores after their husbands died. This is so unnecessary. But it illustrates how wide-spread the "All Flash, No Cash" mentality is, even among leaders.

A MANUFACTURED IDENTITY

In each of these examples, there is a consuming desire to build and sustain an image that wins compliments and applause and an objective to establish an identity through visual excesses. Diana Crane speaks insightfully on the subject when she says, *"Human beings use clothing to create and control their identities."* I would add to that, cars, cosmetics and other accessories. All of us can relate to her findings to some degree because we know and recognize people everyday by their apparel. A policeman, fireman, a nurse, a pilot, all of these individuals obviously utilize clothing to establish and control their identities. In a subtle yet poignant way, their apparel says, "I am this and you are that." These dynamics are also true for others. For example, how does a thug dress? How does a prostitute dress? How does a soldier dress?

If we think about it, each of us uses our wardrobe to testify and signify our preferred identity on various levels. This is not necessarily negative, except for the times clothes are used to create an identity that is not one's reality. This is the case of far too many African Americans who are intent on establishing images of success, wealth and power before any are actual realities. Manufacturing such an identity requires a commitment to extravagance that is too expensive. The dangers inherent in this pathology are serious. It leads to the undoing of so many who can least afford it.

BEYOND PERCEPTION

Identity is not necessarily who we are, but how we wish to be known. Our wardrobes give us the power to control how we are perceived—especially since man looks on the outward. Therefore, by selecting certain brands of clothes and other visible trappings, we can declare ourselves to be rich while poor. We can portray prosperity while we are in poverty and promote an identity of one who has it all when we actually have very little beyond what is on our backs. Of course, establishing and protecting such an identity requires consistent consumerism.

Following Ms. Crane's reasoning, our commitment to extreme external extravagance is indicative of a major identity crisis among blacks, one that is based in and inextricably linked to the ingrained inferiority complex we referred to earlier. Our collective pathos is typical of a people who are more familiar with poverty than with prosperity, struggle than success, being victims more than being victors. We are more accustomed to surviving than thriving. This is our common history and despite the strides we have made, far too many of us are still living this nightmare. Even those who have managed to climb into the middle-class, a feat quite commendable given the odds, are only a step or two out of poverty. It is important to note our historical socioeconomic plight is not merely a matter of money. Rather, it is directly associated with our history in America as a race. Unlike other ethnic groups who come to America poor, in search of opportunity, we arrived in America on clearly different terms. We were not brought here with the intent for us to find opportunities and/or prosperity.

This is not simply more whining by another black man seeking sympathy. I want to make a point which requires an understanding of our context that contributes to the emotional and psychological dispositions of blacks out of which flow the destructive "All Flash, No Cash" behavior.

RACE AND RESOURCES

Most of us are familiar with what it means to be poor and powerless. We know the feeling of being disregarded and disrespected on the basis of race and resources—and have experienced the chill of bigotry, prejudice and racism. We know all too well the reality of being excluded.

All blacks can relate to the fact that we have existed in America as a traumatized people. We have been trivialized and to a great extent, trapped. We are acutely aware that our common plight of continuous struggle (because there are a few exceptions) is directly related to two things—race and resources. Of course, race is the prevailing reality. Although some blacks foolishly seek to forget their blackness, it remains a permanent fact. The point is, it is the natural tendency of a person or people who have been so long rejected, disrespected, disregarded and excluded to seek ways to change this demeaning state of existence. This is especially true when it is evident that your indigenous group is not the majority in power. The result brings a sense we are inadequate, inferior and insecure.

These are the conditions which fuel the insane competition among blacks, commonly referred to as "the crabs in a bucket" syndrome which is one of the primary reasons blacks are doing so bad. We are madly competitive against each other. Out-doing and out-performing gives us a sense of pleasure, power and distinction within the culture. We are proud to say, "I am the only black with a position like this, a house like that," etc. This is why when it appears that one among us is about to climb to another level, we yank them down as quickly as possible. It is also the reason those who do manage to achieve some success are hesitant to reach out and give a helping hand to another black. First, it is risky because the persons you try to lift may be intent on pulling you back down.

Second, so many of us enjoy the prideful feeling of being the "exceptional negro." This is the individual who brags about being the first or the only black to have or to have accomplished a certain thing.

YOUR TRUE NET WORTH

We also strive desperately to win the approval, acceptance and favor of the race in power. This is done in multiple ways, one of which is through identities created by our external representations. Aware of the fact that people are more likely to accept you when you look like, sound like, dress like, drive like and eat like them, blacks set out to accomplish this by all means necessary. It matters not who or what we neglect in the process—and it is immaterial how painful it is or how pricey.

We are obsessed with the pursuit of being considered a black who has arrived—which lets us into the circles where blacks are few and far between. Seeking to impress drives us to reckless financial stewardship, and we become blind to the limits of our budgets.

Keeping up with the Jones' is a dangerous game. My mother

and father instilled this lesson in our heads as children: "Be yourself and don't be overly impressed with what other people have." They taught us not to envy or be jealous. "You don't know what they did to obtain what they have." They also taught us not to determine our sense of worth by our clothes, cars and cosmetics.

Obviously, many did not hear or receive this lesson. Please understand, actual net worth and perceived net worth are seldom the same. Countless African Americans concentrate on building an image based on façades, rather than creating actual wealth based on facts—and this is precisely what keeps us powerless in America and the world. Being overly consumed with flash is an exercise in futility and leads to calamity. This means amassing materials that depreciate and only have short-lived attractiveness. It is imperative that blacks shift our thinking to pursuing actions which build net worth. A dramatic change in mindset has to be taught and caught.

You build net worth, not through your rolling stock (cars) but through your growing stock (investments). You improve your net worth, not through bulging clothes closets but through full bank accounts. You increase your net worth, not through designer fashions but through diversified sources of incoming funds.

DO CLOTHES MAKE THE MAN?

Overcoming the "All Flash and No Cash" mentality requires knowing yourself, loving yourself and your intrinsic self worth. Only then can you be freed from the slavery of living to be accepted, approved and applauded by others, on their terms. Too many African Americans exist in this state of emotional, psychological and financial tyranny. When you discover your true God-given value, you will no longer need materialism to feel good about yourself. *"Clothes don't make the man; the man makes the clothes."* You can apply this to any category.

- Vince Young wearing a football jersey means he's at work and being paid millions. James Dixon in the same jersey means—zilch!

- Tiger Woods wearing a red Nike shirt on Sunday means he's in the hunt to win a major championship. But for thousands of others, it means they are dressed fashionably and are probably 20 strokes over par!
- Beyonce, wearing a sexy garment on stage means she is working to sell another million CD's. But for countless others, it means they could possibly catch a cold!
- Bishop T. D. Jakes wearing a distinguished custom tailored suit means he is preaching to thousands and reaching millions. But for so many others, it means their house note won't be paid on time and they will not be able to retire at a reasonable age.

"Clothes don't make the man." Say it again!

A GENERATIONAL EPIDEMIC

When you know and love yourself, you will not rely on external appearance to define you to others and certainly not to the point of destruction. Then you will be able to focus on building real net worth rather than perceived net worth.

For blacks, this is a generational epidemic. Black children learn too soon the difference between Keds and Nike. Early on they develop the crippling mindset that they are only as beautiful and valuable as is the popularity and price of their clothes and other items they can show off. Unfortunately, they inherit this mentality from their materialistic parents and it is reinforced daily by messages through multimedia. It is sad to see parents pass the issues of low self-esteem, inferiority and insecurity on to their children.

Once this mentality is embedded in the spirit and psyche of today's youth, they are almost destined to live the rest of their lives building fronts rather than solid fiscal foundations. Too many become the innocent victims of the issues of their mamma and daddy; parents who seek to impress other people through the way they dress their children; with their expensive tennis shoes, designer dresses, jeans and jackets. Unfortunately, most of these parents have no focused commitment to making the education of their child a top priority. They invest heavily in their feet but hardly anything in their head! How many of these same sharp children, have a set of encyclopedias or a computer? How many are exposed to Hooked on Phonics or attend academically enriching programs? Have these parents established a scholarship or education fund for their children? Brands names don't get you into college, brains do!

At the end of this book you will find my recommendations for instilling economic stability into the minds and hearts of the coming generation.

It is never too late to change.

CHAPTER FIVE

WE ARE LOCKED UP AND LOCKED OUT!

*The notion of going to jail being a badge of honor
is stupid and insane. Promoting doing time as some sort
of "rite of passage" into manhood or gangsta-hood is
devious, deceptive, demonic and destructive.*

The late W. Leo Daniels, a minister in Houston, published a sermon entitled, *"What In Hell Do You Want?"* Today, I am asking a similar question of all of our young men and women, and our youth, who are following in the footsteps of the foolish who were so smart they ended up behind bars—locked up and locked out. *"What In Prison Do You Want?"*

The only destination I can think of worse than prison is hell. It is the only place where such a vast population of the wicked will congregate, unable to exit.

Over the past 25 years, I have made more than enough visits to jails, prisons and detention facilities. From the first until the last, they all have one thing in common. They have made me sick. No matter who the inmate was: a friend, a church member or a blood relative; it did not matter. Whether it was a male or female, someone who had pled guilty or innocent, it made no difference. Each visit to any correctional facility has left me with a feeling in my gut that I cannot adequately describe. In one short phrase…I hate it; not because I have a weak stomach. (I can handle a morgue rather than a prison.)

I have never been able to get used to seeing humans in a cage. It is a portrait which remains difficult for me to process. What a ghastly sight to see a person who is made in the image and likeness of the Divine, reduced to the lowest degree of disgrace and humiliation. To see a man exist in a state of confinement suitable only for untamed animals is a disturbing paradox.

I do not mean to suggest that I don't understand the need for confinement, because I do. Obviously, we have to be able to protect the innocent from those who threaten the well being and safety of others, and if it is necessary, to protect some people from themselves. There is also a need for punishment which discourages people from continuing a life of crime. I agree there has to be clear and unpleasant consequences for law breakers. All of this is understandable, yet I find it degrading and depressing.

SO WHAT'S THE LURE?

Why so many people are voluntarily in line to go to prison is perplexing to me. To wake up everyday knowing your planned agenda will eventually lead to handcuffs, a police car, a courtroom and a cell block is more than irrational, it is insanity.

Prison is a place of enormous contradictions. It is an institution where many die and some come alive; a place of the guiltless and the grieving; the rebellious and the remorseful; a place where darkness and light seek to co-exist; where experience and inexperience cohabit. It is filled with victims and victimizers; those in immense pain and those who no longer feel pain; the super intelligent and the woefully illiterate; those who dealt drugs and their addicts; individuals who prey and those who pray; those with hope and others with no hope at all; those possessed by demons and those who have been delivered. It is where many come to their senses and many more lose their minds; of sinners and saints; where the devil is at his worst and God is at His best.

Prison life means exposure to abnormality, indecency, obscenity, profanity, immorality, inhumanity and vulgarity. So what is the lure? This is the question being asked of those who display the propensity to repeat the tragic mistakes of incarcerated forerunners. Do they want the danger, the depression, the disease, the degradation and the dehumanization? Are they drawn to the fighting, the manipulating, the raping, the surviving, the compromising or the exploitation? What's attractive—the beatings, the gang warring, the will-breaking, the guards gaming, the sexual perversion, the grown men crying or the old men dying?

Think of the questions as a multiple choice exam. Circle one. What in hell (I mean, prison), do you want?

AN ENDANGERED SPECIES

Over 200,000 (some estimate 290,000) prison rapes occur each year. Hundreds of gangs exist behind bars, warring for respect, turf and other things every day. The number of beatings and fights which occur daily are innumerable.

Every person in prison is an endangered species. This is why I am on a mission to rescue those who are presently candidates for incarceration and to strengthen the wills of those who are presently caught up in the system to work toward release, vowing never to return. Why? Because it is impossible to talk about rescuing black America without addressing the prison problem. I don't just mean talking, lamenting and complaining. I mean actually being prepared to do something. I am, hopefully you are too. If not, I pray that after reading this book, particularly this chapter, you will be ready to act.

One thing is certain, should the present trends continue, the black race is sure to become a "has been..." a "used to be..." an anathema. We are presently well on our way to being a by-word in this nation—and are definitely an endangered species. All of this is due to the enormous rate of blacks, particularly black *men,* who are caught up in the federal, state and local correctional systems. This rate is so alarming that every individual, agency, organization and institution, which claims to have an interest in the state of black America, must dedicate time and resources to understanding, addressing and alleviating the crisis.

We need a 10-year strategic plan based on a bold vision to

reduce the prison population by 30% and 50%, over the next 20 years. These are aggressive goals but they are achievable. At the moment, no such plan exists nationally which is embraced by the black church, key organizations (NAACP, Urban League, 100 Black Men, fraternities) or political groups such as the Congressional Black Caucus, and entertainment groups. We need a vision we can communicate to the masses in unison and a plan we can execute through our varied mediums and multiple methods.

Within three years, every black family, every black child should understand and rehearse: "I am not a candidate for prison." I'm going to college; EDUCATION over INCARCERATION!" This needs to happen for the reasons we are discussing in this chapter. The new vision and plan needs to also be embraced by professional black athletes and entertainers through existing or newly formed organizations.

Until now, no such concept has been cast for black America to buy into. I am asking you, the reader, to join me in advocating this goal. We can't afford as a nation and certainly not as a race to continue to lose the large percentage of human capital represented in the prison population. In addition, we can't afford, as a nation, the mounting tax bill!

PERCEPTION VERSUS REALITY

All Americans are aware that we have a problem, yet most are unaware of the magnitude of the matter. Many would rather stick their heads in the sand and pretend it doesn't exist. But I urge you to pay close attention to the data and contemplate the ramifications.

According to the U. S. Bureau of Justice Statistics for 2005 (www.ojp.usdoj.gov/bjs), over 2 million individuals are incarcerated in prisons or jails at the federal, state or local level—and the number keeps growing. If you add those who are either on probation or parole, the number exceeds several million.

Here is the most devastating detail: whites are imprisoned at the rate of 709; Hispanics at 1,857; and blacks at the astounding rate of 4,682, per 100,000, in our population!

What this means to blacks as a race is that too many of us are "locked up, and being locked up also means being locked out!" Digesting these staggering statistics and deciphering what they truly mean makes it difficult not to be alarmed. All Americans should be motivated to get involved. However, if no one else says or does anything, every sober-thinking black person should begin spreading the message of anti-crime and anti-incarceration and we must hold one another accountable for living the message.

The facts above clearly illustrate the disproportionate number of blacks (male and female) who are either in correctional facilities or under penal supervision. These numbers are used to substantiate the nation's and the world's perception that blacks are generally more criminally inclined than are whites and other races. This conclusion is easy to reach if the only informational sources consulted are the daily news and the stats we have just reviewed, which are published by creditable sources.

However, when we consider other data which requires digging a little deeper, this perception might be altered.

For example, the fact Bakari Kitwana provides in his book, *"The Hip Hop Generation"* which is based on statistics gathered from reliable sources enables us to view this problem through different lenses. They will broaden our understanding concerning the inequities within our system of law enforcement and the nation's penal system. But do not jump to the inaccurate conclusion that I am about to give justification for blacks who commit criminal acts and go to jail. This is not my position. On the other hand, if we are interested in the truth, we have to consider all relevant facts, even though they seldom make the evening news, and are generally kept out of forums for public consumption.

Kitwana explains the impact of the 1984 Crime Control Act and the 1984 Sentencing Reform Act, both of which can be traced to earlier laws which dealt with sentencing for drug related and conspiratorial crimes. These acts are the basis for mandatory minimum sentencing guidelines which has resulted in more convictions and longer sentences for violators, even those not associated with violent crimes.

LOP-SIDED NUMBERS

The following statistics reveal what America's War on Drugs have actually accomplished and how disproportionate the arrests and drug related incarceration percentages are between: whites vs. blacks. For example, according to U.S. Justice Department figures, 13% of monthly illegal drug users are black, and 74% of monthly illegal drug users are white. Think about it. Since these facts are known, why are the incarceration numbers so lop-sided? From 1985-1995 the incarceration rate for blacks increased 707%, but for whites the number only escalated 303%.

IS IT EQUITABLE?

Let's consider why these disparities exist.

One reason is the difference money makes. That is, white illegal drug users tend to have more discretionary money than their black counterparts. Meaning, they can pay for more expensive drugs and support their habits without having to commit the kinds of crimes, non-violent or violent people of lesser means often commit to support their addictions. These crimes obviously are quite inflammatory and make for sensational news, which shapes public opinion, drives legislation, resulting in more street level arrests and longer sentencing based on minimum guidelines.

Another factor is due to health insurance which covers treatment and rehabilitation programs that are administered in private facilities. Due to economic disparities, more whites are able to send their drug addicted family members to these programs (hospitals) than blacks. So white addicts are more often treated as patients while black addicts are more often treated as criminals. Most black drug addicts have to rely on publicly funded treatment programs, which these days are hard to find as a result of funding cuts. Due to changes in public policy, the number of these facilities has been reduced and those that do exist are often underfunded, thus understaffed and inadequate.

Still another sad reality is the fact there is more than sufficient evidence of corruption in our beloved nation's criminal justice system and that the drug trade in America could not possibly be as lucrative as it is without the cooperation of powerful people in high places. At the street level too, there is more that goes on than honest policing. People who read beyond the headlines of newspapers understand this. Unfortunately, most Americans are too busy or too lazy to do any serious research and investigation on their own.

One other factor that has to be considered is the cost of legal representation. When most blacks are arrested, the matter of economics really works against them. For the most part, blacks have to depend on state appointed counsel. Obviously, this is a gross disadvantage—and again it is tied to money. Consequently, they either have uninformed, underinformed and misinformed opinions of the crime and incarceration phenomenon.

For instance, have you personally looked at racial profiling data? Or, do you care? Those who have, understand the inequities of this toxic practice. It also involves neighborhood profiling. This means that while local law enforcement agencies should work to address areas of high crime in communities which are heavily populated by minorities, resources should definitely be allocated for addressing crime, particularly drug related criminal activity in suburban neighborhoods. Of course, these communities are often heavily populated by whites. Studies prove that illegal drug use is higher in the *burbs* than it is in the *hood*, due greatly to monetary access among youth. But arrest and incarceration rates do not reflect this reality. This is why informed blacks remain cynical, suspicious and often disrespectful of our government and law enforcement. It is why many conclude that justice is not meted out equitably.

THE CRACK INVASION

Be assured, none of the above information or observations should be misconstrued to suggest that criminal behavior of blacks is excusable. The fact that more whites than blacks are involved with illegal drug use (and I need to add drug trafficking and money laundering) than blacks, does not make the blacks who are involved at any level, less guilty. This again is the point made by Cosby in his well known speeches. Blacks cannot use the inequities in the system as justification for illegal and self-destructive behavior, which also destroys our communities and endangers our culture. However, the other side of the debate seeks to declare the fact of the blatant injustices within our system which should not be ignored. Further, it is important to explain why the unprecedented increase in black incarceration rates is still happening.

The invasion of crack created a new generation of street level drug dealers, intermediary pushers and neighborhood and city level kingpins. This invasion also produced a new breed of addicts. Crack is a most toxic blend of cocaine and brain-diminishing chemicals and can be purchased in small quantities. The combination of easy accessibility, low price, ultimate but brief euphoria and highly addictive nature makes it extremely destructive. This new form of illegal drug trading associated with crack resulted in a river of cash flowing in urban and rural communities unlike anything ever seen before. It also produced greater levels of violence that became necessary to enforce the rules of the crack gangs.

Further, the crack epidemic birthed a new populous of addicts who became criminals to fund their addictions. And it produced a mass of victims who were no longer capable of going to school, holding a job and raising children.

DREADFUL IMAGES

Those caught in the wicked web of crack addiction or the world of drug trading became criminals in various forms and varying levels. Many streets are littered with images of the "walking dying" all hours of day and night, always searching for another hit on the death pipe. Having no means of funding their sickness resulted in burglaries, robberies, and other kinds of immoral and unlawful activity. The media fed on this phenomena and filled as many minutes as possible with stories of crimes, testimonies of victims and the arrest of both addicts and dealers. The fear struck in the minds of Americans by these dangerous and dreadful images became the impetuous for what came to be called America's "War on Drugs."

This argument is substantiated by reports published by Human Rights Watch Report (United States—Punishment and Prejudice:

Racial Disparities in the War on Drugs), the Substance Abuse and Mental Health Services Administration, the National Criminal Justice Commission and the U.S. Justice Department.

Kitwana alarms us with the fact that from 1965 until now, the U.S. prison population grew from 200,000 to the present 2 million plus. All sources report there are approximately one million black males entangled with the criminal justice system at some level today.

THE NUMBERS DON'T LIE

The major growth of prisons happened during the 1980s and 1990s, and continues—and is greatly contributed to by non-violent drug related offenses. According to Mary Barr, the National Institute of Justice and FBI reports that 85% of those incarcerated in local, state and federal facilities are substance abusers (www.conextions.org/html/drugs.html). .

We need to understand that blacks, who make up about 12% of the U.S. population, account for 13% of the nation's monthly illegal drug users. On the other hand, according to the U.S. Census 2000, whites make up 77.1% of the total population and account for 74% of monthly drug users. Do not forget these facts.

Let me be clear, this should not be a "black people be proud" statement that we only make up 13% of drug users. That we do, is actually a cause for great concern. However, it is an effort to present a real picture, and to put a factual face on the problem.

Since these are the actual numbers, there are several questions to be asked and addressed. First, why does the image that comes to mind when most Americans think of drug users and addicts appear as a black face? It is due to the thorough job the national and local media did in the 1980s and 90s. Every day, these reports of high crime were aired, showing our nation and the world the faces of young black males and hip hop generationers associated with crime related to the crack cocaine epidemic. Thus, society's perception of an illegal user is a young black man in a back alley, rather than a white male in a suburban setting.

Every day in the news there were reports of rising drug use, crime and arrests and nearly always it was someone black in an urban environment as the subject. Then, there were the reality "cop shows" that only work the streets of the poorest areas in American cities. Day after day, we were shown through various forms of media that black youth in the hood were using and selling drugs, and committing violent crimes that terrorize neighborhoods and cities. This was done sufficiently to vilify the image of the young black male. Think for a moment: have you ever viewed a police reality show where doors in middle class or elite suburbia were kicked in and the persons arrested for drugs were white?

Feeding on the fear frenzy, politicians took the message of being hard on crime to their campaign soapboxes. They began campaigning on "toughness on crime and zero tolerance" delivering speeches and making promises to punish criminals severely. Soon new measures sprouted and hastily crafted legislation began to be drafted, resulting in the acts, already mentioned, adopted by Congress which enforced mandatory minimums and longer sentencing requirements. Gripped by fear and frustration, the public supported these measures almost without question. And politicians who could be labeled "soft on crime" were ousted.

ADDRESSING THE DISPARITIES

Since the information shared in this chapter is public knowledge and all media including the talk shows on radio and TV have research teams that certainly have access to the same statistics, why don't we hear about it?

It is obvious to many that a conscious decision has been made to misrepresent the reality. Could it be that these and other eye-opening facts are kept quiet to protect the reputations of some while destroying the reputations of others? To publish the 74% vs. 13% statistic would have to lead to corresponding police and judicial work. Again, someone knows who and where these illegal drugs users are. They also know what drugs are being purchased and from whom they are being bought. And for some reason, our nation chooses not to arrest and prosecute them under the laws currently on the books. Could it be that mandatory minimums were created and intended for one segment of society?

The Human Rights Watch report (May, 2000), states the following: *"With this report Human Rights Watch seeks to bring renewed attention to extreme racial disparities in one area of the criminal justice system—the incarceration of drug law offenders, i.e., persons whose most serious conviction offense is a nonviolent drug law violation. The high rates of incarceration for all drug offenders are cause for concern. But the grossly disparate rates at which blacks and whites are sent to prison for drug offenses raise a clear warning flag concerning the fairness and equity of drug law enforcement across the country, and underscore the need for reforms that would minimize these disparities without sacrificing legitimate drug control objectives."*

Presently, one out of every 20 black men over age 18 is in state or federal prison compared to one out of every 180 white men. That there is, at the least, indirect discrimination evidenced in the information you have now processed is difficult to question. Hopefully, this nation will again be challenged to address and rectify existing disparities. But only an informed and ignited public can make this happen.

A Lethal Combination

In my personal opinion, there needs to be a massive education campaign designed to inform all Americans about the disproportionate number of blacks who are arrested and handed long term sentences for non-violent drug crimes versus their white counterparts. The inequities in this biased system of justice are quite apparent and raise concerns pertaining to the morality and constitutionality of the present way we arrest and prosecute non-violent criminals. The fact is, the larger number of users are the least number arrested and convicted. Something is wrong with this picture!

Many believe the arrival of crack in black neighborhoods, the adoption of such rigid and inflexible laws and the imbalance in how certain crimes are viewed and prosecuted, are the results of a sinister scheme. It is believed that the goal is to diminish if not destroy the black race.

Whether intentional or not, the consequences of this lethal combination are all around us. I once heard it said, "Blacks not only get prosecuted, we get *persecuted* by the system."

Another believable and substantiated theory has to do with what is often referred to as the "prison industrial complex," which alludes to the rise of private corporations who build and operate complete prison units or provide significant services. Prison is big business—and arguably one of the fastest growing industries in our nation. The vast revenues circulating through the local, state and federal penal system and its connecting parts are ever increasing. There are so many aspects to it and so many businesses that feed on its existence. Who can calculate all the money spent on legal fees, law enforcement, investigative work and the many other elements that depend on crime to succeed? There are theories that those who profit from prison revenues, in the private and public sectors are only interested in its continued growth. This is not the case for all, but it is believably the case for many.

CHEAP INMATE LABOR

The revenues generated by private sector contractors serving the prison industry is ever escalating. We spend between $35 to $40 billion in taxes annually to support prison construction and operations. There is a serious list of companies who compete for opportunities to contract with government to build and provide all sorts of services to local jails and state and federal prison units. Kitwana provides a thorough list including Cornell Corrections, Correction Corporation of America and Wakenhut Corrections Corporation. These are private sector companies that are in the prison operations business. They are all taking economic advantage of the constant flow of blacks and browns being housed in corrective custody.

There is also the growing trend of prison labor being utilized by private industries. This is cheap inmate labor that is being hired out by companies such as Konica, IBM, Dell, Toys 'R' Us, Honda and Compaq for as little as 20¢ per hour. In most cases the pay is dimes on a dollar. These companies that participate are able to replace workers who would earn $8 to $15 per hour with cheap, relatively free, labor, driving their profits up by driving labor costs down. Prisons are now looking and functioning more and more like slavery plantations.

Go ahead and picture it. A white guard being called "Boss," watching over a group of black men whom he calls "boys" or worse, working to produce products for a "privately owned" company, while under the state's supervision. It has been called, "Slavery in the 21st Century." Many feel this is what prison is about—and why the arrest and prosecution rates between blacks and whites is so unequal. Can you imagine the inmate population being majority white and the system functioning like this? The very thought should be alarming.

WHO'S GETTING PUNKED?

Herding black men and others in and out of prison creates a cash cow which is never deficient of milk—*green* milk—and everyone nursing is constantly full. From commissary products, to soap, to toilet tissue, people are cashing in on crime. More bluntly stated, whites are cashing in on black crime. We get charged; they get a check. We go to the commissary to send their grandchildren to college. Our skyrocketing incarceration rate pays everybody but us. This is why I ask those who continue to line up to go to prison, "Who's getting pimped? Who's getting played? Who's getting punked?"

Too many brothers just don't get it. Getting caught up in the prison system is not only personally detrimental, it also ruins the potential of the race. Think of what one million working, voting, focused black men could do economically, politically in communities and in families. You cannot support FUBU and Sean John locked up. You cannot influence who represents your neighborhood, sets public policy or leads the nation locked up. And you cannot protect and preserve your community locked up.

A million brothers behind bars translates to a million brothers leaving our most valuable resources, our children, to be taken

91

advantage of and neglected. Without fathers and community dads, our kids become easy prey to all that is evil, including the vicious streets and a system which is often void of sensitivity and already planning for them to fail.

A million black men locked up leaves at least one million black women to be cared for, protected and partnered with to continue our cultural legacy. The absence and limited availability of employable, stable men has also contributed to a reduction in black marriages. Our reproduction rate is at an all time low, partly because our men are locked up and locked out. The Biblical admonition, " be fruitful, multiply and subdue the earth," is impossible when one out of three black males in their prime, child-bearing years is entangled in the penal system.

Then there is the long-term affect of so many black males spending so much time in the demoralizing, debilitating and diseased environment.

The truth is, it takes a miracle to spend years locked up in a system that is programmed to destroy your sense of dignity, sacred selfhood, self respect, personal confidence and manhood, and come out healthy, sure of who you are. This is why so few do and are unable to start over and become productive upon release.

THE POWER TO SAY "NO"

Tens of thousands of brothers exit prison and return to their homes, neighborhoods, families and significant others, disturbed, depressed, diseased and disillusioned. And, there are practically no programs provided to accurately diagnose these cases before or post-release. Neither are there dollars to adequately fund treatment services by healthcare professionals, including emotional and mental healthcare providers.

These men are left on their own to fend for themselves and the unbearable burden falls to them, their families and communities who are not capable of sufficiently addressing and remedying the problem. Prison becomes the only place many are capable of dying in.

We can debate the conspiracy theories until the end of time and may never reach an agreement on what is true and false. But on this, there can be no debate. An alarming number of black males and a rising number of black females are caught in the web of the penal system; in fact, 1 out of 3 black males between 19 and 29 are in some form of custody today. These statistics are eating away at our viable presence in the earth.

We should also agree on this, black brothers and sisters, we have the power to decide against a life of crime and drugs; negative socioeconomic conditions notwithstanding. We still have the power to say "no" to the temptation of quick, dirty, deceitful money and to an artificial high which fries brain cells, ruins futures, wrecks families and debilitates neighborhoods. Indeed, we have the responsibility.

As a minister, I can tell you hundreds of stories of men and women who have seen their lives permanently changed through a spiritual transformation combined with a personal commitment to live by godly principles. I also believe it can happen for millions more.

NOT A BADGE OF HONOR

The demonic tactic to which many have become prey has certainly set our race back because when you are locked up, you are locked out. Imprisonment results in being locked out of the lives of those who really love you; family and friends. It means being locked out of a job, out of your dreams, out of an entrepreneurial vision, and out of the political process. In a nutshell, it means being locked out of making a contribution and counting as a spouse, parent, a son or daughter, a neighbor, a friend, a worker, a leader, or a voter.

This is the message I am seeking to convey. We need every black person to count for us and, yes, to help make this nation a better America and our world a better one for our children and grandchildren.

Correction or Punishment?

Interestingly, while I was writing this chapter, I sat in a 24-hour breakfast restaurant overnight and at about 4:00 A.M., three Texas Department of Criminal Justice prison guards came in to eat. I thought…how ironic. They were traveling on one of the buses used to transport convicts from Houston to the prison units along the I-45 corridor.

Something within urged me to walk across the dining room and invite myself to their table, which meant interrupting their conversation. So I did. I introduced myself as Pastor James Dixon, hoping that might cause a tempered acceptance. Their faces bore an unwelcome look and although they agreed to talk with me for a couple of minutes, it was clear I was being tolerated.

I asked them their opinion concerning the growing prison rate and about the attitude they confronted among this generation of inmates and what the possible answers to the crises might be. Their responses were quite clear.

"My take is, they don't want help and actually, they see going to prison as a rite of passage and wear it as a badge of honor" was the first comment. Another one stated more passionately, "I don't think prison is a deterrent anymore. They don't get worked hard enough. Frankly, they used to work 'em from sun up to sun down and it was hard labor. Some of it was barbaric, I admit. But it was hard and made you not want to be there or return."

Then, when I asked about the cure and whether enough was being done to facilitate rehabilitation, the tone changed. "I don't think anymore can be done. And I don't believe these people want to be rehabbed. It's gotta come from within the person." And then came this statement, "Look at all of these black males, they don't care and they don't want to change. There is nothing you can do about it. Remember when Ann Richards was Governor here in Texas? Her thing was treatment and rehabilitation. All that money she wasted. It really didn't change anything."

Ann Richards was our state's last democratic governor before George W. Bush was elected. The two had completely different philosophies about prison. When Mr. Bush was elected, he changed the name of our system to the Texas Department of Criminal Justice. Prior to that it was called the Texas Department of Corrections. One stood for correcting while punishing and the other promoted punishment for criminal behavior.

It is still being debated as to which philosophy is the best approach to the problem. Perhaps a blending of the two is in order.

A REVEALING CONVERSATION

It goes without saying the funding pattern also changed. Treatment, education and rehabilitation dollars dried up. Many community-based drug treatment facilities closed due to financial crisis and addicts were left with nowhere to go but…you guessed it, back to prison.

The conversation with the prison guards was insightful and frightful at the same time. It was revealing because it gave me a look into the minds of these fully-seasoned veterans of the system. They were convinced black males were not worth any greater investment than the cost of a cell and bare necessities. That was my sense. And had they been talking among themselves, there's no doubt they would have been more explicit. Not one mentioned any bright reports of some inmates showing promise and potential.

It was frightening because they made it clear that even my questioning and evidenced interest was not welcome or encouraging. I mentioned that I was trying to work from the outside on what they were dealing with on the inside. But there was no sign of any appreciation for my efforts. For them, correction was not a realistic consideration and rehab would be a waste of dollars.

Once back at my seat, I motioned for the waitress and paid for their meals in advance of their knowing—a sign of appreciation for their time. When they approached the cash register they were informed I had picked up their tab. Two of them did not acknowledge the gesture at all. They exited without even a nod or a smile. The third, however, hung back, and said, "Thanks." I walked over to him showed him the cover for this book, shared the project and he said, "God bless you."

I could not help but think of the thousands more young black boys who are in juvenile facilities now, and are on their way to the penitentiary unless there is a drastic change. And I thought of the thousands of black men who are in court and in county jails waiting to be herded onto that bus in chains. I trembled in disgust at the thought. These are our brothers and our sons.

UNEDUCATED AND INCARCERATED

Now let's really get real! Who is truly getting pimped, played and punked? This is the question every self-proclaimed and would-be thug, street hustler and dope slingin' player needs to be real about. Just be straight up. This is my message to my brothers and sisters who are dancing down the road to destruction.

On the streets, brothers are selling someone else's dope to their own brothers, sisters and friends; destroying them physically, mentally and emotionally and ruining their own community. So now your Mama can't be safe in her own house anymore. Eventually, they get caught with maybe one or two rocks in their possession and a few bills in their pocket. And because they had a gun, they get 10 to 20 years. Both you and your addicted homeboys end up locked up and locked out, uneducated and incarcerated. You were too smart to stay in school, go to college and start a career. Both the addicts and the dealers are now walking around calling other men, mostly white men, "Boss." A few days ago you proclaimed yourself as "Boss." Now you are put in a position where you sound so much like a slave.

Look, I am not trying to shame you…I'm only trying to shake you into reality. Wake up! Stop helping others to destroy us. And stop destroying yourself, then blaming others for it. You are far too valuable for us to lose. It is up to black men to rescue the black community from our predicament of peril, but we cannot do it locked up and locked out!

DEVASTATED AND DERAILED

I believe that in the 70s, just as we were about to make our collective move toward real power, those who feared our plural potential changed the game plan. We were moving forward and upward rapidly. With the increase in college graduates, the rise in black elected leadership, the increase of black middle class paying jobs and businesses, the handwriting was on the wall. We were just about to beat the odds by becoming a real force to be reckoned with in America.

Coming out of the 60s, we were set to take our rightful place at the table of brotherhood. In the 70s, the future still looked promising. Then all of a sudden…we derailed.

The crack cocaine epidemic swept every neighborhood in black America. Urban and rural communities were devastated as our boys became agents of the enemy; turning them against their mamas, daddies, friends and God. Two decades later—millions of addicts later, millions of convictions and legal costs later—we are drained but we are not dead yet. We must act now!

This is a call from the heart of a brother who is not a racist, but a black man who remains proud to be black. It is a call from a man of faith who dares to believe against the odds. It is an appeal from one who is thankful to see every man as a creation in the image of God, to recognize that we each have the responsibility to push one another to pursue our highest, not our lowest self. Therefore, this is a cry for each of us to rise above our self-centered interests and not be blinded by short-term instant gratification at the expense of the whole.

SOMETHING IS FUNDAMENTALLY WRONG

Each of us must become warriors of a nobler kind—who take up the fight to reverse the tragic trend of our 30-year past by unlocking cells, by unlocking our minds and hearts to learn, think and love.

Remember, slavery concerned more than race; it was about money. As you examine the facts concerning the outsourcing of prison labor, you will more than likely arrive at a similar conclusion. As I told one group recently, "If this does not look a lot like slavery and doesn't disturb your conscience, think again!"

Whether you're black, white or other, Catholic or Protestant, Jew or Muslim, rich or poor, Democrat or Republican, you should know that there is something fundamentally wrong with this system. First, think of the jobs being taken from law-abiding citizens, most of whom are low wage earners to begin with, many who are single parents, minorities and persons who are struggling to get on their feet. How can you justify taking work from those who can least afford it? This is certain to result in more crime, more arrests, more convictions and more...slaves.

Second, we are all aware of how difficult it is for ex-offenders to find gainful employment when they are released, especially while they remain on parole. It is next to impossible—and perhaps hypocritical. While locked up, these same people can work for these companies for 50 cents an hour, but when they return home, they cannot walk into a business with a felony conviction and be hired, not even at minimum wage. This holds true for those who have served time for non-violent convictions.

Third, there is simply no way for this kind of system not to breed increasing corruption. Why? Because it means that the more criminals who serve longer sentences, the more profitable it becomes for private enterprise. The fact is that those who invest in and operate prisons for profit also contribute heavily to political campaigns. This creates an environment which encourages corruption.

When I had this discussion with other people, while this book was in progress, their responses, for the most part, have been similar. Most were surprised, appalled and alarmed. There were three questions which surfaced continuously, "Why didn't we know this before now?" "What were we doing while all of this was happening?" And, "What can be done about it now?" Perhaps you are wondering the same thing. I'll attempt to provide answers to these questions,

First, although this information is on public record it is not public knowledge—because it is not generally disseminated. Mainstream media has not made it a priority, neither have legislators or the community. And unfortunately, most of us do not pay attention to what is happening to convicted criminals because we totally disconnect our realities from theirs—"They deserve whatever they get" is the basic attitude. This leaves them completely vulnerable to the few who have personal interests.

Second, while the prison population quadrupled, sentencing laws changed and new operational policies were established and philosophical shifts took place, we were all busy, doing our own thing. Only in small settings, mostly among those who work with penal, legal and juvenile justice organizations, and among activists, were these conversations taking place. It is not a conversation that the black church, fraternities or sororities entertain. Please understand, I am not an advocate for babying criminals; nor do I think prisons should be hotels. But I do believe every offender is due basic human rights. And, when they are violated, it becomes the responsibility of conscientious, God-honoring people to demand that the basic rights of all are protected.

Third, we blindly trust the system to work humanely on its own. This is a gross mistake in judgment. Even with all the evidence that the penal system is flawed, we still tend to trust it to work while we do not watch it. One would think that with all the overturned cases due to DNA evidence, proof of inmate abuse, etc., the public would be more attentive. But this is not the case. Truthfully, it is not difficult to forget about people who have assaulted, burglarized, stolen, sold and used drugs and murdered; hurting people and terrorizing neighborhoods.

WE ALL HAVE A ROLE

Black leaders of various organizations and genres were then, as they are now, functioning without a unifying vision—disconnected from each other and committed to isolated agendas. Obviously, most of us are not lifting our voices to sound the alarm; neither do we challenge the system to function properly, equitably and humanely. We do not facilitate debates and discussions with policy shapers, demanding answers or recommending changes.

So while we were preoccupied, these changes were made, new policies were drafted and implemented, laws were enacted and sentencing guidelines were placed on the books. Profits generated from the new "slave labor" grew tremendously. Mind you, each year our religious organizations have conferences and conventions and never address this crisis. Our national civil rights and justice organizations have held annual meetings and it has not been adequately addressed beyond the usual rhetoric. No action agendas followed.

This is quite embarrassing to admit in an age when we are so blessed with such an impressive roster of black leaders from diverse disciplines. This is the America of Al Sharpton, Jesse Jackson, happened in the America of T.D. Jakes, Juanita Bynam, Creflo Dollar, I.V. Hilliard, Charles Blake, Oprah Winfrey, Paul Morton, Jackie McCullough, Bill Cosby, Kathy Hughes, Kwesi M'Fume, Vashti McKenzie, Noel Jones, Maya Angelou, Michael Eric Dyson, Tavis Smiley, Montel Williams, Maxine Waters, Cornell West, Colin Powell, Lee P. Brown, Anthony Evans, yours truly, James Dixon, II and certainly others who are proven leaders. You see I've learned we all have to take ownership of our condition and responsibility for addressing and resolving our problems. Those of us who are less popular cannot hide behind those who are of celebrity status. Get up and do your part too!

While all black leaders have addressed this issue in one form or another, what we have not done is developed a plan that includes stated positions on critical matters and measurable objectives to be achieved by all who have roles to play.

I applaud programs such as found at the Carol Vance Unit, a division of Texas Department of Criminal Justice in Sugar Land, Texas. The founders of the program understand that one's theology informs his or her sociology. Thus far, the program has proven to be highly effective in reducing the recidivism rate and is preparing felons to become productive citizens.

This experimental program is spiritually based and seeks to rehabilitate felons utilizing classic biblical principles. It teaches inmates to view themselves as creations made in the image of God with divine likeness. It also instills core ethics which impacts the individuals's civic responsibilities.

Many have been doing some good things, perhaps even some great things, but one thing is clear, we were not doing enough together. Actually, there has been quite an effort to distinguish and distance ourselves from each other. So much sparring between intellectuals has taken place; too much fighting among ministries; an abundance of quarreling between politicians; ongoing word wars between activists and scholars. These kinds of behaviors have been our downfall because they have consumed far too much of our attention, drained our resources and distracted our focus from the main thing; loving, lifting and leading our people to nobler heights.

AN UNHOLY UNION

Consider the following facts: because of "The Three Strikes and You're Out" policy, young people are entering the criminal justice system and while they deserve punishment, it is difficult to get out. Then there is the fourth grade test which determines the state's future investment in children. This is why reducing funding for Head Start and other early childhood development programs helps generate children who more than likely are candidates for incarceration rather than education.

There is also the parental failure factor. First, the failure to understand what they are up against. Second, the failure to literally fight from day one to determine the profiles their children will fit into.

Parents who are not sufficiently educated do a great disservice to their sons and daughters. Also, community and church leaders who are uninformed are not in a position to empower their constituents and congregants. So the normal rhetoric continues.

IT TAKES COURAGE!

Black children are born with lots of ground to make up. The color of their skin means they are automatically considered for the negative list. And there are more strikes against them if they are birthed and raised by a single parent where no man ever shows up on their behalf. This is of no disrespect to motherhood. It simply conveys the fact that the presence of a father figure has great value. Unfortunately, expectations are lower for kids without it. If they reside in a certain neighborhood and are a black male, the outlook is even bleaker because investment follows expectation.

Even though our children start out behind, knowing what we are up against is not cause for quitting. We cannot become despondent and discouraged to the point of giving up. It is actually cause for greater determination, discipline and diligence. This is why African American parents must be willing to fight for their children if they are to succeed.

If this means battling for quality schools, for safe neighborhoods, and fighting to overcome and negative stereotypes, so be it! Borrowing James Dobson's book title, "Parenting is not for Cowards!" This is where we have to admit that the playing field remains uneven. Admittedly, it is better than it used to be, but still not level. It takes courage to raise children, especially equipping them to win against the odds. It takes courage, character and commitment to persist and to continue pressing toward the prize.

DOUBLE THE EFFORT

Black parents have to help their children understand early on the fight we are in as a racial group. They have to know that we are battling to strengthen and elevate our race and in doing so, we will make our nation and the world a better place. Former generations of African Americans made sure their children understood this—and taught their sons and daughters that they had to be *twice* as good.

This meant studying twice as hard in school to excel in academics and working twice as hard to learn a skill to become resourceful. It also meant being twice as careful to avoid getting into trouble with the law. And, unless we multiply our efforts to return to this orientation, we will never catch-up. When you actualize the "twice as hard orientation," you can't be denied, overlooked and so easily mistreated and misrepresented.

Former generations believed in and taught the concept of being a credit to our race, which meant going to school and earning good grades, becoming employable, being guided by moral standards, being able to speak intelligently and always looking presentable. Today's word is "represent."

It is the mindset new African American parents must return to. Today's lazy, unfocused and undisciplined brand of parenting plays right into the game plans of those who are eager to profit from our children's failures. But we are smarter than this—aren't we? We *should* be, because our grandmothers and grandfathers were. When they raised children, the playing field was even more unfair than it is today. But they refused to think of themselves as victims and instilled in their children the kind of values, ethics and disciplines that were necessary to overcome obstacles and break through barriers.

These are exactly the attributes this generation lacks, which is why they value materials over morals, diamonds over dignity and selfish gain over societal good. Our entire culture has become heavily narcissistic, characterizing the age and ME-ism, materialism and hedonism.

CALLOUSED AND RESENTFUL

What makes the 21st century brand of self-centeredness extremely dangerous is that worse than a "me first spirit," it projects a "ME ONLY" spirit. Of course, this way of thinking drives the ruthless and reckless commitment to "financial gain at any cost," and to physical pleasure in its lewdest forms, even at the expense of sacred selfhood and the destruction of human dignity.

It is the indoctrination of this sadistic value system which has produced a generation that is not only calloused toward voices of concern, reason and wisdom, but is also resentful towards the messenger of a purer and better way. This is why it is so difficult to motivate today's youth to change their course. You would think seeing enough tragedy and death would do it. You would think knowing enough people who are locked up and locked out would do it. But to the contrary, for every one who goes to prison for druggin' and thuggin' there are 100 more lined up behind them to take their places.

When pleasing self is your only goal, there are no limits to what you will do. When money is your master, you are its slave and will do the most destructive and degrading things to have it. This is why the Bible says, *"the love of money is the root of all evil."* Hence, we see at the street level, the car jacking, drug dealing and robberies. Incidentally, this is also why we see money laundering, drug trafficking, embezzling, fraudulent accounting and dishonest reporting at the corporate level. And on that note we are...

LOCKED OUT OF THE MAINSTREAM

It doesn't help that we live in a time filled with reports of corporate corruption, revealing the vast number of white collar rogues who too are so driven by greed they are willing to lie, cheat, and steal to secure their great grandchildren's silver spoons; ruining and wrecking countless people's lives in the process. The constant report of polluted politics exposing evidence of bribes, the influence of special interest groups and corrupt connection with drug warlords, has tremendous influence on our youth's thinking.

This helps to fertilize the thoughts among our children (who are more informed than they are given credit for) that the only way to really make it in this America is to have an illegal, dishonest hustle. On the contrary, the other American way, "go to church, go to school and get a job" is all a farce. These kids believe that honesty and integrity only lead to poverty, and to make it big you have to be willing to cross the line, whether you are on the streets wearing baggy jeans, a jersey and bling, in a 50 story tower, or wearing a dark blue business suit.

It is the conclusion of this generation's street-smart youth who are competent on current events, especially negative ones, that they are systematically locked out of America's mainstream path to upward mobility and economic elevation. They understand the game of allowing one or two minorities to slip through the cracks every now and then, creating the perception of equal opportunity. They know well the differences between being born black versus being born white in America. They know that equality remains an illusion.

TRICKED, TRAPPED AND TRADED

Although most youth have not read Andrew Hacker's *Two Nations: Divided and Unequal* or *Black Robes, White Justice* by Bruce Wright, they know intuitively, instinctively and/or experientially that they are often under siege before they ever commit a crime. Because being born black in America is to be born a suspect and a target. This awareness is often used as an excuse to do poorly in school or to quit, to be thuggish, commit crime, not to vote or hold a job. But this is a mentality we must seek to do away with. It reveals a victim's complex.

The bottom line is, too many blacks who think this end up locked up and locked out. It's a mind game. *"As a man thinks in his heart, so is he."* Parents, and all who have a hand in raising and developing youth, have to fortify their minds with knowledge that empowers them to succeed against the odds, rather than being in denial about the situation.

To fight back, we must begin with knowing and telling the truth. And it is our responsibility to make sure all black youth understand and are held accountable for their actions. We have to expose the facts about crime and its cultural consequences, dispelling the notion that being a criminal is cool. We must publicize the reality that the homeboys and "dawgs" in prison have been tricked, trapped and are being traded to profit others.

This means any black man peddling drugs has to be viewed and treated as a traitor and a punk who is being pimped by the enemy. Any black man writing and producing poisonous content and selling it to our youth is a betrayer and we have to demand a change in content. We want to be successful, but not at the expense of our children's self-perception and worldview; not at the expense of promoting misogynistic views of our women.

Black youth who refuse to be educated have to be checked because we understand the price of black illiteracy is simply too high. Any black man who refuses to work, has to be isolated and privileges of fellowship and courtship should be forfeited. He is a poor example for our children and a burden to our economy. We have to teach our girls and our women how to recognize and motivate, but not tolerate, brothers who refuse to try. We must do our part to reprogram the thinking of black men about being responsible, resourceful and respectful preservers of the race.

Righteous Action

My message is that to much of our wealth is locked up and locked out.

- Think of our artists, chemists and scientists who are locked out.
- Think of our activists and politicians who are locked out.
- Think of our artisans, builders and craftsmen who are locked out.
- Think of our teachers and preachers who are locked out.
- Think of our doctors, bankers and lawyers who are locked out.

Too many of our resources are languishing behind bars or otherwise entangled in the penal system, unable to make a contribution commensurate with their God-given gifts, skills and talents.

I admit there are obstacles in our way and conspiracies designed to derail and destroy us. I acknowledge that our nation's progress with regards to racial equality is yet incomplete and leaves much to be desired. But I am also aware that an unrighteous response is not the solution. History counsels us well if we listen. It teaches us that a righteous cause followed by a righteous action is ultimately too powerful to be denied. It is how we overcome.

Cowardly Behavior

Dropping out of school, selling poison to your brothers and sisters, playing on people's addictions and ending up in prison is not smart, neither courageous. Robbing innocent people at gunpoint is not a courageous act. This is cowardly behavior. Going back to prison repeatedly as expected by the system is not courageous. Making excuses for insidious and illegal behavior is for cowards. Don't get courage and bravery confused. You can be a brave fool, but having courage requires character.

Winners are those who possess courage to overcome obstacles of any kind. This has been the history of blacks in America and around the world. If you want to look into the face of courage, find some brother who, in spite of the system, overcame through education and determination and made it to the top. Find a sister who did the same. We are out here; we are not weak, and didn't sell out—and are still proud to be black. We fought hard to get here, helped some others on the way, and are fighting everyday to hold on to what we have, and other days to gain another yard. But we're always in the battle.

For those who wonder why children of this generation will do anything to anybody, and why there is such blatant disregard for pain, theirs or anyone else's, here it is: The values that are being instilled in today's culture, particularly the black culture, encourage jackin', smokin', pimpin' and playin'. Those who have been (and are being) indoctrinated with this fatalistic philosophy are prime candidates for prison. Unless they are caught early by observant parents or other conscientious and competent caregivers, they will become a statistic in the system. They are being raised to be criminally inclined long before a crime is ever committed.

DEMONIC DISCIPLERS

Everyone knows parents must become more involved, but what does that mean? Well, for starters, it means knowing and identifying the sources of sadistic indoctrination. These are found in all forms of media; TV, movies, CD's, DVD, Internet and print. Each of these mediums publishes, promotes and pays demonic disciplers. What's that? It is a person who proclaims and portrays a message that desensitizes us to iniquity, glorifies ignorance, and justifies illegality.

The hip hop culture is filled with such figures whose faces are as commonplace with this generation as was The Jackson 5 in the 70s. Michael, Jermaine, Marlon, Tito and Jackie influenced everything from our fashion, to dance, our hair and our conversation. Only, they never cursed. They were not grinding girls who were barely dressed or popping them on the butt. In fact, most of the music we listened to was romantic, but not sexually explicit or illicit. None of it encouraged crime, violence or vulgarity. Now, the most profane and dehumanizing images and messages are pumped into the heads of our youth though mainstream media. The craziness shown on BET and MTV has taken the place of Soul Train.

NO SHAME OR REMORSE

Today's version of demonic disciplers knows no boundaries. They advocate violence, decadent drugs (the use and trade) and every other evil imaginable and unimaginable. They need to be addressed and challenged to change. Why? Because they are profiting on our problem and are no better than the persons who are behind the scenes controlling the drug flow or those who are manipulating the system to make prison profitable for themselves.

The role demonic disciplers' play in the whole process is psychological. They are the "mind conditioners" who brainwash millions and indoctrinate them into a cult of loyal followers on a path that only leads to death and destruction.

How else do your explain a wave of youth who knows no shame, feels no remorse, who considers going to prison, being beaten, manipulated, labeled, raped, pimped and marginalized to be a badge of honor or to prove their thug authenticity.

SET FREE!

Perhaps you think the word cult is too strong. Well, let me try and help you.

Earlier, we mentioned the common mantra of those who are being discipled by these dark forces is "Thug for Life." To show you how deeply this has been ingrained, even at the funerals of their fallen friends, T-shirts are worn, often displaying the dead person's picture, who typically has been violently killed. These shirts frequently bear the slogan, "Thug Til I Die!" (They mean it literally.) This is the kind of fatalistic pledge that people in cults make. It resembles the brand of insane loyalty of suicide bombers who are members of Al-Qaeda. This is why the prospect of being locked out of the mainstream, going to prison or even dying early does not discourage or deter these devoted disciples. For them, even their dead friend's corpse, riddled with bullet holes, stretched out in a casket, is a tribute to THUGGIN'.

They gather, always in large numbers, to pay honor to a life briefly lived. Often the dead thug has left behind a young wife or woman with children to figure out how to explain daddy's death and take over his responsibilities. You would think such a scene would be enough to spark a spiritual rebirth and decision to change. But too often it does not. To do so would be viewed as dishonoring the long list of fallen soldiers who went out "Thuggin'."

If this is not cultic, I do not know what is. Of course, I expect to be challenged regarding my opinion, especially by those who are doing the demonic discipling and those who are converts of this wicked way. Those involved don't want to face reality. I hate having to say it, but it is what it is—and only the truth has power to free us.

The problem is, so few people know the truth and fewer are willing to proclaim it. A good God is not behind this kind of behavior. It can only be the work of the devil. Love is honest. And it is time for us to be honest with ourselves about our situation. This word is to all my brothers and sisters who may be challenged by this message. Just know it is out of love that I speak the truth. Locked up and locked out is not where we belong.

"You shall know the truth and the truth shall set you free."

CHAPTER SIX

THERE'S POISON IN THE PANTS!

Facts are facts. Blacks lead the statistics in sexually transmitted diseases and particularly in HIV/AIDS infections, and we are dying at a faster pace than other racial or ethnic groups. This has to be dealt with, not ignored; because you cannot cure what you do not confront and you cannot change what you are afraid to challenge.

He's tall, always neatly dressed in business attire. His skin is smooth, his voice is strong and his body is firm from the three workouts per week. He is built like an athlete with a pronounced muscular physique, accented by a well-defined "six-pack." His foreign sports car is *normally* clean. He knows all the classy spots to dine and the right wine to order. He lives in a swank high-rise apartment and everything about him announces "first class." This man has no apparent bad habits and above all else, goes to church every Sunday and listens frequently to gospel music.

He is so close to the description of the man a girl's mother told her to hold out for and the kind she has dreamed of since she was young. But what her mother did not know to tell her was to "beware, there could be poison in his pants!"

This is precisely what happened to a young woman named

Precious Jackson, as detailed in the Washington Post, February 7, 2005.

She described the love of her life as, "A very fine black man. Six feet two with an almond-milk complexion, dreamy dark eyes and a deep voice."

During their nearly two years together in Los Angeles, he was the sunshine of her existence, even though he had a habit of landing in jail and refused to use a condom when they made love.

"I didn't ask him any questions," Jackson said. "I didn't question him about his sexual history. I asked if he had been tested, and he said one test came back positive but another one came back negative. I was excited to have this man in my life because I felt I needed him to validate who I was."

He seemed as honest as he was charming, even telling her about his crack-cocaine habit, and frequent arrests. Looking back, she now wonders if he picked up another habit in jail, where men have sex with other men, by consent or by force. She wonders if he was one of the many African American men who hide their sexual orientation from others in the homophobic black community, a conspiracy of silence called the "down low."

"HOW COULD YOU?"

In 1998, Precious Jackson's boyfriend was arrested for drug possession and taken to the Los Angeles County Jail, where he underwent a routine HIV test for inmates entering the system. A short while later, a letter was delivered, telling her he tested positive and that she should immediately be checked out.

Her positive result arrived in May, 1998. "I was 26. I was shocked. I was stunned," said Jackson, who is now an AIDS activist working for a Los Angeles treatment center called Women Alive. "A lot of emotions went through me. I was sad. I was angry at myself because I got caught up. 'Caught up' meaning I was so into keeping this man at all costs."

Precious Jackson said other people are responsible, too. She tells the women she counsels at Women Alive to take charge of their health, by whatever means. People cannot be trusted, she emphasizes—something that became clear recently when she ran into her old boyfriend.

"He's out now," she said. "When I told him I was diagnosed, he apologized, said he was sorry, and that he didn't mean for this to happen. It was actually cool to see him…until he kept talking. He said he had two more kids," Jackson recalled. "That's when I got mad. I said, 'How could you?'"

He answered that his girlfriend didn't want to use condoms—even though she knew he was infected.

A DEBT OF GRATITUDE

Apparently, Precious is not alone. Tragically, she is one of a growing number of black women whose lives are forever altered by the discovery that the same penis which provides pleasure can also provide poison. The fastest growing population of Americans with HIV/AIDS is not white homosexual men, but African American women!

For this reason, much of this chapter is deliberately written to sisters. Although there is a need for all segments of our society to become more knowledgeable about this disease and to be more responsible with their lifestyles and the choices they make, I want to talk with black women directly.

You have played such a unique and important role in the progressive evolution of our race—and our history is what it is because of the contributions you have made. Although deserved credit has not been amply published and accurate appreciation has never been given, the world owes you an unmatched debt of gratitude.

It is also true that black women are owed an apology. Why? One glaring reason is because 68% of all new HIV cases are African American women and African American men have the most to do with producing this sad statistic.

Reports from the Center for Disease Control are available for public knowledge. I would encourage every African American to spend time on their website (www.cdc.gov) digesting the statistics

113

which relate to our health, particularly with regard to the HIV/AIDS pandemic.

ALARMING STATISTICS

According to the 2000 U.S. Census, blacks make up nearly 13% of the U. S. population, yet comprise nearly 50% of the 1.1 million presently carrying the HIV virus in this nation.

To be specific, of the HIV/AIDS cases diagnosed during 2005, African Americans comprised 49%; whites 31%; Hispanics 18%; Asian/Pacific Islanders 1%; American Indian/Alaska Natives less than 1%.

Of the states reporting in 2001-2004, 18,849 persons under age 24 were diagnosed. Of that number, 11,554 (61%) were African American. Of infants prenatally infected with HIV, 65% were African American.

A SCOURGE OF DEATH

To say this disease is a challenge for us is a gross understatement. Former NAACP president, Bruce Gordon, made this comment concerning the impact of AIDS on the black community, "Simply stated, let's not say this with fancy words: HIV/AIDS is killing our community. It's killing us."

He is right. According to a report published by the international AIDS charity AVERT (www.avert.org), since 1981 when AIDS was first identified, "more than a half million Americans are believed to have died" of the disease. Thirty-eight percent of these deaths were among African Americans.

In 2004 AIDS became the leading cause of death for African American women between the ages of 25 and 44 according to Jennifer Kates of the Kaiser Family Foundation (www.kff.org). In fact, more blacks die annually of AIDS than any other race.

The Center for Disease Control (CDC) and Preventions reports the rate of diagnosis for African American women is four times the rate of Hispanic women, and 23 times the rate for white women.

How are so many black women being infected with HIV? Well,

there are three methods by which the virus is primarily transmitted: blood transfusions, intravenous needle sharing, and through sexual encounters with men.

This leads to a need for understanding the trends of black women being infected. Consider the following: by the end of 2005, it was determined that 66% of black women living with AIDS became infected through heterosexual contact, while 31% of them were infected through drug use, and only 2% through blood transfusions.

A Dangerous Path

Studies indicate that the rate of Asian and Pacific Islanders (women) with AIDS is 2.8 per 100,000; for Hispanics, 15 per 100,000; for whites, 22 per 100,000; and for black women, an astounding 58.3 per 100,000. Now remember, most of these cases come through heterosexual contact with black men (CDC Fact Sheet, April 2006).

One thing that makes my flesh crawl is to see a sister holding hands, hugging and hooked up with a man who is obviously gay or bi-sexual. I am probably voicing something a million other men would say "Amen" to. It deeply upsets me to see a woman who has positioned herself to be deceived and led down such a dangerous path.

Unfortunately, this is not rare in the black community. It is becoming more and more an *abnormal* norm. And for the most part, it has gone unaddressed. If you attend a family reunion, a concert, take a walk through a mall and certainly if you go to church, you are likely to run across these odd couples. They look more like two girlfriends than they do true sweethearts. It is worse when they are married and even more tragic when there are children born into this union.

My heart goes out to sisters who end up in these twisted relationships. For one, it is physically dangerous due to the health risks involved. These men, who use women to create a façade of authentic masculinity while maintaining ties to the gay world that is based in illicit sex, expose themselves and their women to deadly diseases.

Such relationships are emotionally dangerous because a man who is bisexual is in a confused state himself and cannot possibly nurture a woman's emotions. In fact, he has to play on her feelings to keep her entangled in his wicked web. If you talk with women who have been in these relationships they reveal how emotionally traumatic such experiences are. There will often be symptoms of depression, anxiety, and wrecked self-esteem as a result, making it difficult to recover.

Most do not seek spiritual or professional counseling because of shame and fear. They often bear the behavior of females who have been abused or raped. This is because, in a real sense, they truly have been violated. And what makes it more embarrassing and sad is that they allowed, facilitated, supported it and even fought for it.

EMOTIONS CLOUD REASON

So the question is, how do so many women end up in relationships with men who are obviously effeminate? Sometimes it is plain denial. Other times it is desperation. Often, it is a combination of the two. Normally in these cases, others close to them notice the signs and caringly express their concern. Often this causes a rift in the relationship because it is information they don't wish to hear. Women tend to resent those who tell them the truth about men to whom they are emotionally tied.

Too often women allow themselves to feel before they think. And when feelings outweigh thinking the results are normally disastrous. Emotions cloud reason. Feelings won't allow you to see what you really see, hear what you really hear and know what you really know.

Sisters, when someone cares enough to honestly give you a heads up about a man who they perceive to be effeminate, don't go on the defensive. Listen! Slow down! Take a step back so you can consider the evidence from an emotionally safe distance. Now be honest with yourself about what you see. Look at his walk, the movement of his hands, his voice tone, the way he stands, the way he sits, and the way he dresses. Check out his friends and associates. Are they obviously masculine or not? Are there signs of femininity? Where does he hang out, and with whom?

Most straight men will tell you we are extremely uncomfortable in casual conversations with effeminate or homosexual men. We do not prefer their casual company or an environment where they frequently gather. This does not mean we are homophobic or paranoid. Rather, we do not relate well to men who are so unlike us, yet are still men. It is awkward, to put it mildly. I mean, what do you talk about?

Remember the old adage. "If it walks like a duck, quacks like a duck, look likes a duck, chances are...IT IS A DUCK!" It would be better to err on the side of caution.

DESPERATE FOR LOVE

The number of black women who are enduring an agonizing aloneness is extremely high. The ratio of available strong, stable, straight, spiritual men to available women of the same description is out of balance. Again, this is another sensitive subject our community is going to have to confront head on. It has serious ramifications.

Agonizing alone causes many sisters to unknowingly become desperate for attention, affirmation and affection from the opposite sex. It is why so many women are willing to overlook the obvious, ignore the advice of trusted relatives and friends and get romantically, sexually, emotionally and even matrimonially involved. It is amazingly frightening to see what some will put themselves through to get a man, any kind of man, and what they are willing to overlook and tolerate to keep him.

Compromises made for the sake of companionship makes them susceptible to self-endangering situations. This is in no way limited to but certainly does include committing to relationships with men who are obviously bi-sexual. Remember, the statistic 46% of men who have sex with other men are infected with the HIV virus.

In light of this reality, we have to urgently do more to help address the deceitfulness of bi-sexual men and the lack of discernment. What is the cause?

A primary reason is the outlandish number of girls who are not being raised in a home with a strong man as a father and role model. It is well proven that girls need the masculine nurturing of a man who loves them during their developmental years. Their beauty, uniqueness and self worth needs to be affirmed by a male who wants nothing from them other than love and respect. They need the care of a father and/or a small network of men who are not interested in their bodies, but who helps them appreciate and develop their spiritual, emotional and intellectual selves.

Girls who do not receive this on their development journeys are more likely to become desperate and vulnerable to any man who shows up to fill the long existing void.

Another reason is a matter of *definition*. Young girls need to know what makes a man a man—and need to be raised by strong men. I'm not speaking necessarily of physical strength, although that too is important. Girls need to grow up knowing what a real, strong man looks, sounds and acts like. Every girl needs to observe mannerisms and other masculine qualities. It is said that when most girls mature, they begin to search for their fathers in potential mates. Unfortunately, too many are looking for something they have never seen.

THE "DOWN LOW" PHENOMENON

The next group of women in the large number of those who contract the virus are *not* desperate. They understand masculinity by definition and generally make what appears to be sound decisions regarding men. They expose themselves to the life-threatening disease HIV due to the lowest form of deception. They contract the disease from black men who are on "the down low."

In his New York bestseller, "On The Down Low," J. L. King opened the eyes of many about the phenomenon of the growing number of black men who have sex with other men, while maintaining relationships with women. These include female dates, girlfriends and even marriage partners.

According to King, these "down low" brothers fit into a few

basic categories. In his chapter on DL Behavior Types, he lists and discusses the Nature Brother, the Thug Brother, the "I Have A Wife/Girlfriend" Brother and the "I'm Just Curious" Brother. He explains their distinctive profiles but is careful to point out the factors which unite them. One, they are all involved with women on some level; two, they are all sexually involved with men; and three, they are all deceivers.

Unlike men who are professed homosexuals and professed bi-sexual, brothers on the "down low" are masters at camouflaging their dark sexual identities. They do not display the warning signals of men who are visibly effeminate.

In fact, these men are anything *but* feminine. They are portraits of the kind of man women are looking for in a straight man. According to King and others, these brothers have the perfect fronts:

- They dress, walk and talk masculine.
- They do the things straight men do and go places we go.
- They are in school or college, they work, have businesses, and hold leadership positions.
- They enjoy sports, they work out and even go to church.
- They are often all a woman's mother and grandmother told them they deserved.

Yes, they are the kind a girl gladly brings home for dinner. What's not to like? But what females and families who become attached to these men have no clue of is their well-concealed life away from them. This is described to be a sordid life; an underworld where men exchange sexual favors often with more than one man, then return to their wives, girlfriends, and families to be with them in every way befitting a straight man.

This is more than scary, sad and sickening—it is also satanic. There is no justification for this kind of deception. The collateral damage of such behavior is immeasurable. The toll on families, the women and children involved is too great and the severity of the health risk is indescribable. The degree of deception required to practice the DL lifestyle leads me to change the label from "Down Low" to "Low Down." Every brother who is into this perversion needs to be faced with reality and get their life together!

An alarming number of African American sisters are being infected through sexual encounters with African American brothers. Rather than uniting together for the purpose of reproducing life, which is the plan of God, in too many instances, black women and men are coming together to reproduce death. This is the plan of the devil who seeks only to steal, kill and destroy.

COMPOUNDING THE CRISIS

Let's digest this disturbing reality: black men who have sex with other men, (BMSM) are found to be a great percentage of HIV virus carriers and transmitters to African American women.

According to the Center for Disease Control, of the male adults and adolescents diagnosed with HIV/AIDS during 2004, the cause was: male to male sexual contact–65%; heterosexual contact–16%; injection drug use–14%; male to male sexual contact AND drug use –5%; other– 1%.

Clearly, the leading number of transmissions among all men is male to male contact of those who admit to homosexuality and to being bi-sexual.

The same report cites those numbers by race and ethnicity. Consider the following facts for 2001-2004 which exposes the percentage of men who have sex with other men (MSM) who were diagnosed with HIV/AIDS. White men—43%; black—39%; Hispanic—9%; Asian/Pacific Islanders—1%; other—less than 1%.

Additional reports reveal the alarming numbers of BMSM who are not only carriers of the HIV virus but, even worse, are unaware of it.

These facts put African American women at a tremendous disadvantage and make them high-risk candidates for HIV infections. Of course, these BMSM represent a few different categories. But when you add to BMSM the other contributing groups, black men and women who are not committed to monogamous relationships and who engage in casual, unprotected sex, the crisis is compounded. In this day of extreme sexual liberation what is participated in as fun has the potential of being fatal.

AN UNPLEASANT CONFRONTATION

Blacks need to face some very embarrassing facts and accept responsibility for changing patterns of destructive behavior. Sexual promiscuity is out of control in our community. This is not to suggest at all that other races are sexually *in* control. Indeed the sex revolution of recent years which promotes complete sexual freedom has influenced every race, culture and community. But this book is addressing the plight of blacks. Statistics inform us we are literally pleasuring ourselves to death!

Of course, this is a challenging subject to discuss because of the prospect of sounding stereotypical, labeling blacks as immoral and giving no African Americans a medal for high ethical or moral behavior. This is not the point. *"All have sinned and come short..."* But we cannot continue to be overly concerned about whether or not we are more or less in order than others.

THE DEMOGRAPHICS

A nationwide study (2005) conducted by the CDC reveals that black high school age students were more sexually active than others prior to graduation. The percentage of students who said they had engaged in sexual intercourse by age 18 were as follows: black, 68%; Hispanic, 51%; white 43%.

It was found that African American girls were more likely to have had sexual relations with older men than other girls in their peer group. Our young women are looking for something in these relationships which was missing in the home.

Epidemiologists say the spread of HIV is attributable to socioeconomic and demographic conditions specific to many African American communities. Black neighborhoods, they say, are more likely to be plagued by unemployment and impoverished conditions. In these areas, schools are underfunded, joblessness abounds, drug use and alcohol consumption are skyrocketing—so too is the arrest rate. These dynamics are common in neighborhoods that fit the profile just stated.

"WE SHOULD BE VERY AFRAID"

The high incarceration rate in these neighborhoods results in a ratio of women to men that is out of balance. There are too many women, too many children, and too few men—and even fewer men who have never been in jail. For many of these black men, prison is an expected stop on their journey, an accepted part of life and several terms in prison is not out of the norm. Of course, the HIV rate inside of prison is estimated to be 8 to 10 times higher than it is outside.

For black women, the result has been devastating, said Debra Fraser-Howze, founding president and CEO of the National Black Leadership Commission on AIDS. "We should be very afraid," she said. "We should be afraid and we should be planning. What are we going to do when these women get sick? Most of these women don't even know they're HIV-positive. What are we going to do with these children? When women get sick, there is no one left to take care of the family."

Fraser-Howze says the number of health facilities in black communities is inadequate when compared with the growing size of the problem. Officially, Washington has been slow to respond, continues Fraser-Howze, a former member of the President's Advisory Council on HIV/AIDS under President Bill Clinton.

"Reducing HIV infections among black women will involve more than appeals to avoid risky behavior, asking women to remain abstinent and passing out condoms," observes Adaora A. Adimora, an associate professor of medicine and an adjunct Professor of Epidemiology at the University of North Carolina at Chapel Hill.

You also have to eliminate the economic factors that dramatically influence behavior, disease and risk. Living conditions are "critically important" to fueling the spread of the disease. Communities influence "social networks, partner choices, likelihood of marriage, types of risk behaviors, as well as the consequences of risk behaviors." Adimora goes on to say, "Black women are not more promiscuous than other groups of women, but they are the least likely to be married of all women because most live in communities where men are more scarce. A 22-year-old woman who has sex with multiple men she meets in an area with very low HIV prevalence, such as a Georgetown bar for well connected young people in DC politics, probably has less chance of getting infected than a 22-year-old woman who had sex with only one man in a poor D.C. neighborhood with a very high HIV prevalence."

HIGH RISK BEHAVIORS

As black men cycle in and out of jail and prison, black women are torn from the family unit and go on to have "more concurrent relationships," or more than one partner in communities where more people are infected, according to an article, "Social Context, Sexual Networks and Racial Disparities in Rates of Sexually Transmitted Infections," written by Adimora and Victor J. Schoenbach, an associate professor in UNC's school of medicine (Journal of Infectious Diseases, Vol. 191, 2005).

"Incarceration directly affects sexual networks through disruption of existing partnerships," Adimora and Schoenbach write. Black men entering prison are placed in an environment with "a pool of individuals among whom . . . high risk sexual behaviors, HIV infection and other sexually transmitted infections are high."

Among prison inmates, HIV infection is estimated to be 8 to 10 times higher than that of the general U.S. population, they write. But health experts can't point to any study of male sexual preferences before and after prison sentences, or in behavior once outside, Adimora says. Even if they could, "...imprisonment and promiscuity in black communities are not the issue. The socioeconomic conditions that lead to them are."

AIDS AND THE BLACK CHURCH

While doing the homework required for this chapter, I became thoroughly convinced the black church should repent—and it owes an apology for sins of commission and omission that have contributed to the proliferation of HIV/AIDS in our community and the world. Those of us who are a part of the leadership construct of the church have done far too little to address this national and global pandemic; the number one health crisis facing blacks in America and beyond.

According to AVERT, one in 50 African American males and one in 160 African American females is infected with the virus (www.avert.org/hiv-african-americans.htm). This is frightening to say the least. In all honesty, while some pastors and church groups have done more than others, as a collective, we have said and done far too little. More recently, this is changing through programs such as Balm in Gilead, based in Richmond, VA, led by a wonderful sister, Pernessa C. Seale. They are mobilizing churches and individuals to fight AIDS in the U.S. and in Africa. Every church should consider joining.

COMPASSION, COMPETENCE AND COMMITMENT

First, we need to repent and apologize for our lack of compassion for those who have died and those presently infected. Our unexpressed love for those in our churches and our community has been loudly declared by our virtual silence and inactivity. God is love.

Second, we need to repent and apologize for our lack of competence. So many among us have not taken the subject seriously enough to educate ourselves beyond periodic flashes in the news. Most have not empowered staff or a committee to investigate or comprehend the crisis. Such lack of competence has far reaching ramifications including the inability to speak and teach intelligently on the topic.

Third, we need to repent and apologize for making church too comfortable. Through messages which are accommodating to risky lifestyles, we have made it easier for the people who should depend on us for truth to put themselves at continued risk, without any sense of conviction. We have also added validation to such lifestyles by promoting those who practice them, which increases their influence and inspires more of the same from one generation to the next. I know this is a point of contention, but I am convinced it should be a part of the black pastor's and church's apology.

Also, we need to repent and apologize for our lack of commitment to confronting the AIDS crisis head on. Of course this takes courage—which leaders often lack. In the face of problems as significant as this one, we have a tendency to give ourselves a pass and allow others, like the government, the medical community, social service agencies or even God, to handle it. We side-step the issue to avoid becoming overwhelmed by something else being added to our existing list of seemingly impossible responsibilities.

"And when he saw the multitudes. He was overcome with compassion because they were sheep with no one to shepherd them. They were without help and were being harassed."

This explains Jesus' actions in the face of obvious human crisis, how He responded to the condition of human suffering. *"He went from village to village teaching, preaching and healing all kinds of sicknesses and diseases."* What a powerful portrait—powerful because it was practical and relevant because it was resourceful.

MORE THAN RHETORIC

This is precisely where the church often misses the point. Too frequently, our message and ministry does not address the misery of the moment. It begins with a faulty interpretation, which leads to a philosophically skewed proclamation and results in a non-relevant application. What makes religious rhetoric nonessential is when it does not lead to rescue, remedy, restoration and redemption.

To follow the example of the Christ motif requires all three tenets: (1) speaking poignantly to the issue; (2) giving thorough explanation of the nature, consequences and contributing behaviors to the crisis; and (3) seeking cures and solutions to the problem— all with a goal of saving lives and improving the quality of life for each person in the concentric circle of a faith community.

In too many instances we have ignored, condemned and

125

shunned the problem and the people directly affected. Some of this, of course, has to do with our homophobic concepts and rigid traditions. Just as bad, many have simply been accommodational, providing a comfortable environment for those who continue to engage in practices that are proven to be high-risk lifestyles.

For these reasons, on behalf of the black church collective, I (we) repent and I (we) apologize.

WHAT IS OUR RESPONSE?

In all honesty, this has been a part of the problem. Early on, many AIDS activists were also represented as gay activists. The prophetic side of the ministry could neither embrace them or their message because of the incongruence which exists between the gay lifestyle and Christian doctrine. For many activists who were also gay, this was misinterpreted to mean pastors and churches did not give a darn about gay or sick people, since at that time this was the face of HIV/AIDS. Over the years, as the face of the disease changed, barriers have been removed.

Going a little deeper, it should also be confessed that AIDS was perceived to be a plague confined to the gay community. That is the report the media gave us. The general response of the church was, "Those gays better repent and change their ways."

With great zeal it was proclaimed this disease was a curse which came as a result of abominable behavior. This response obviously angered and alienated people in the gay and AIDS activist's communities. They were expecting and seeking a priestly response, rather than a prophetic one. They are seeking sensitivity, not a sermon. But while the church could probably have done better with communication and building bridges, let's be fair. There are two factors that fueled a more prophetic message. For one, the gay rights movement of the latter part of the 20th century was growing simultaneously with the spreading of AIDS.

Many church leaders were responding to the demands of the movement by proclaiming orthodox Christian dogma (or teachings) about homosexuality. And, while there has been heated debate over interpretation in and outside the church, the Bible still says what it says. Homosexuality, just as adultery, is presented in scripture as a sin. Only, homosexuality is explained in scripture as "unnatural affection" and as "an abomination." To remain loyal to the text, ministers have the challenge of speaking this truth in love, rather than in anger and condemnation.

All medical intelligence has continued to assert that the HIV/AIDS epidemic is contracted and is spreading due to human behavior. It is a condition that reflects people's choices. Certainly, it is exacerbated and fueled by the socioeconomic dynamics already explained. But nonetheless the disease is transmitted through human actions.

This is what dictates the requirement of a prophetic response from the church—and not to expect one would be unrealistic and unfair. It would be like deliberately speeding and appearing defiant when the police officer issues a citation. On the other hand, the fact that people impacted by the disease are sick, hurting, depressed and dying, dictates the need for a priestly response. But such expression is provoked by humility and confession—and this was not the mood of many AIDS/gay activists in the early days. They were adamant concerning gay rights and arrogant about demands. Be mindful, being prophetic without being priestly breeds condemnation, and being priestly without being prophetic is condoning of behavior which often leads to deadly consequences, and that is not love.

No More "Business as Usual"

Perhaps the mean-spiritedness projected by many conservative evangelicals discouraged open dialogue and damaged the reputation of the church. It also hurt relations between the two entities. As we have mistakenly done historically, many black ministers took cues from leading evangelicals whose narrow and prejudiced theology rendered them incapable of being priestly while remaining prophetic. Thus, while HIV/AIDS began rapidly spreading in the black community, we had so distanced ourselves from the problem and the people we viewed to be responsible, that we could not observe the changing of the face of AIDS, neither the pillage it was wreaking on our community. Blinded by stereotypes, prejudices, and phobias, we could not see the crises of HIV/AIDS emerging in our cultural family.

Now that we have been honest about the mistakes of our past and better understand the magnitude of the problem, let's discuss what the ministry role of the black church should be as we go forward.

There obviously should not be "business as usual." The church as a collective is going to have to become a voice for education and representation, and a primary vehicle for change. The thousands of churches that are already on the case and in the fight are to be commended. But this is a battle no black church should view from a safe distance.

To drastically reduce the spread of HIV/AIDS, this has to become a focus for more churches nationwide. The issue has to be aggressively attacked. The 85,000 black churches in America figure prominently in the solution matrix. Our potential impact is huge if we will all commit to doing something practical and meaningful.

First: We need to craft a message of love that does not compromise the truth as taught in scripture but at the same time communicates our compassion for those who are HIV-positive, including those who are in lifestyles of high risk.

Our message must be balanced, addressing behavior and healing. The typical rhetoric is not acceptable here. Pastors and ministry leaders need to begin with becoming informed about the disease, the faces of AIDS and the sophisticated approaches to solutions and treatment. This is where the balance of the priestly and prophetic is called for. Some ministers have been predominantly priestly while others have been strongly prophetic. Those who are priestly major on showing compassion and mercy for persons who have ventured outside of scriptural parameters. The emphasis here is on helping persons to heal and to recover spiritually and emotionally.

On the other hand, those whose message is heavily prophetic are clear to emphasize the connection between the behavior and consequences. They are unrelenting in their deeply held convictions concerning the results unrighteousness surely cause. Either of these positions without the other is out of balance. A more effective message would be both; rather than either/or.

Second: Black ministers and churches must become anointed advocates.

I suggest organizing A.S.A.P. (Anointed Servants Advocating for People). We must unite in our appeal to hold the government responsible for funding research in pursuit of a cure. There must also be increased financial resources for customized intervention, prevention and treatment strategies which must include more healthcare facilities in our communities. Ultimately, the socioeconomic conditions that attribute to the environment many blacks and other minorities find themselves in, have to be addressed. As clearly documented in this text and others, poverty and a sense of powerlessness create a context for all sorts of mal-behavior, including drug abuse and sexual irresponsibility.

Third: Support legislation that requires all persons convicted and sentenced to time in prison to be tested before they enter, annually while they are in, and upon release from prison.

There should be total acceptance and support for this legislation. We should also push for prison reform laws which require the government to make prisons physically and environmentally safe. A reported 200,000+ in-prison rapes occur per year. Experts generally agree that the numbers are actually much higher due to several factors: (1) Many are not reported due to fear of retaliation. (2) Authorities are often knowledgeable, but are in on schemes which pit persons against each other. (3) Sometimes victims are raped multiple times a day or week but do not report each instance. (4) There is awareness by victims that reports will not result in investigation and decisive action.

129

Fourth: Every black church needs to have some form of HIV/AIDS ministry.

Gone are the days for the so-called mission auxiliaries and brotherhood groups that do not address contemporary issues. This is a time for relevant ministry—and how a church could not address the AIDS crises in a deliberate organized and systematic manner and yet think themselves to be relevant is beyond me. To formulate an AIDS ministry means to shed light to our people on the greatest health threat African Americans have ever faced.

Where do you begin? There are many models out there. I strongly suggest conferring with other church groups that have developed working models after experimenting and refining their approaches. The highly-acclaimed Balm in Gilead Organization (www.balmingilead.org) would be a great resource of information and ministry methodologies.

Some programs are prevention-focused and seek to discourage high-risk behavior through education. There are also models which focus on intervention, responding in love to persons who are already diagnosed with HIV. These ministries usually offer counseling services and encourage proper medical attention. This is necessary because without such intervention, people with AIDS are often completely devastated with depression and overwhelmed with grief. They often accept death far too prematurely and, without proper invention, will more than likely engage in activity that exacerbates their condition.

Then there is the health side of this equation. Some church groups have launched aggressive initiatives such as establishing clinics and healthcare facilities. There is a huge need for more to be done in this area, but whatever the angle, whatever the approach, by all means, do or say something. Be about touching the lives of those who are directly affected.

Children are infected and dying. Families are in crisis. There are actions every church can take to show the strength of the love of Christ in the context of the suffering in our culture.

Families must also take responsibility for teaching and educating each other concerning HIV/AIDS and of the negative impact the disease is having on our community. The first responsibility of parents is to protect their children. It is sad so many fathers and mothers abdicate this role of informing their offspring about the danger of premarital and unprotected sex.

No More Denial

As we mentioned earlier, 68% of black high school students admitted to having had sexual intercourse (compared to 51% for whites and 43% for Hispanics). The black students who had sex before high school graduation were also more likely to have had four or more sexual partners.

Other reports indicate that black youth lead in the number of sexually transmitted diseases. Who can measure the extent of emotional damage?

These facts should be a wake up call for all parents (especially African American parents) to become aggressive about educating and protecting their kids. Being timid regarding discussing these matters is not an acceptable excuse. Saying you are too busy is a cop out. And simply ignoring the situation is to admit that you really do not care about your kids' well being.

Believe me, there is a correlation between the behavior of children and who informs them. Unfortunately, most are learning their tips on sex from watching videos in their parents' home. There is no shortage of sexually explicit content in the music and the graphics aired 24 hours a day—and they have captured the full attention of today's youth.

These videos feature sex every way but the *right* way. Scenes with multiple partners, same sex partners and trading partners all abound. Our children and young adults are soaking up these pornographic representations of sex. For many who have been raised in church, Sunday School, or in a family where values and ethics are taught, the orientation they now have about sex from the media is, "Do whatever you please to get your freak on."

Tragically, many of these young, ill-informed consumers of corruption expose themselves to debilitating and deadly diseases trying to simply be cool and accepted by their peers who are also confused.

Kawanza Kunjufu estimates that 90% of male-to-female relationships of sex portrayed on television does not involve a husband and a wife. In my opinion, the number seems even higher. This continues to confirm in the minds of our youth that sex and marriage have nothing to do with one another. The truth is, marriage is the *only* sex which is right, according to the Book.

There is no end to this discussion. But let me say to all of us: Come out of denial. When Bruce Gordon proclaims, "AIDS is killing our community," the cemetery would agree with him.

Do not let your grave testify to this. Get tested. Check your lifestyle —and, with God's help, change what is necessary. We need you around!

CHAPTER SEVEN

OUR BATTLESHIPS BECAME CRUISE SHIPS: THE BLACK CHURCH

Is this historic institution, although more sophisticated, more lucrative and larger than ever, becoming increasingly more irrelevant when it comes to making a defining difference in black America?

In recent times, the black church has been called "a sleeping giant"—and much worse.

My grandparents referred to it as "The Old Ship of Zion." Millions of black Americans love the church, while a growing number despise it. Other blacks are simply indifferent and still others are leaving it, preferring to identify with more cosmopolitan mega or super-mega congregations which are predominantly white and led by white ministers. Considering the historical backdrop, this is a phenomenon which deserves our analytical thought.

Despite the challenges we presently face, I am convinced the black church in America is the most intriguing, colorful, versatile and durable institution on the planet. Line it up against any other organization and they will pale in comparison. I am not speaking of the church in general which could certainly be described in similar terms; rather I am referring specifically to the black church in America.

OUR SPIRITUAL LEGACY

To fully appreciate the truth in the statements and claims I have asserted, one would need both empirical data and experiential knowledge. It is impossible to describe and comprehend the height, depth, breadth and width of the black church's significance in American history and its influence in our culture, unless you have lived it or seriously studied the subject. Those who have are indelibly impacted by the unparalleled record of this institution's affects on the black community, the nation, and the world.

Stop any African American on the street, on a plane, wearing cashmere or coveralls and interview them. If they are honest, their stories cannot be told in full without mentioning the role the church has played in their family's evolution. Somewhere in their family tree is a grandparent, uncle, aunt, mother or father who either took or dragged them to church. Some individual in their bloodline was (or is) grounded in a belief in God. There is a preacher, a mission sister, a deacon, an elder, Sunday School teacher, or choir member in their legacy who gave them a faith foundation. Rare are the exceptions.

Listen to a black athlete when he is applauded for high achievement or an entertainer who receives an award, including most hip hop artists, business persons or politicians; they will all make one statement, "I thank God for my talent and this opportunity." Seldom do we see a movie or read a book about someone black or based on a black life, without the church's prominent appearance. It's hard for us to talk about *us* without talking about our *church*.

The black church's influence and mark is indisputably without equal. Yet, at the opening of the 21st century it is strapped with a label such as "sleeping giant." We have to wonder "why?" and then ask, "Is it warranted?" And, more importantly, what should be the role of the black church in America today?"

Consider these facts:

- There are approximately 85,000 black churches in the United States.
- The estimated combined annual revenue for black churches is $3 billion.
- These churches own or control some $50 billion in assets.

Despite these signs of significant presence and power, the black community is in dire need of leadership, direction, advocacy and vision. And when you consider the present state of black America, the question always surfaces, "What is the church doing?"

PREVALENCE VS. RELEVANCE

Let me say at the outset, the central purpose of the church is to proclaim the death, burial and resurrection of Christ—and that believing on Him transforms lives and prepares people for eternity. However, in this book I am addressing the issues of what the church does beyond teaching salvation to affect contemporary society. How do we actualize what it means to be the salt of the earth and the light of the world?

It is true that black churches continue to be the most *prevalent* entities in any city or town where there are black people. But the question remains: is it still the most *relevant* entity in black life?

In every historically African American neighborhood you are sure to find a few defining landmarks: barber/beauty shops, liquor stores, funeral homes, fried chicken restaurants and churches—lots of them! But by far, black churches out number all the rest. They are everywhere you look, on practically every corner and on the blocks in between. They are in buildings which look like churches; and in storefronts, strip centers, school buildings, auditoriums, hotel ballrooms, and cathedrals. Then there are the mega church campuses with multi-thousand seat sanctuaries, gymnasiums, skating rinks, ball fields and private schools—multi-million dollar facilities that point to the intellectual, financial and spiritual powerhouses these institutions have become.

In every city you can find black churches of all sizes, from 20 to 20,000 members. They represent every denominational flavor: from Baptist to Pentecostal; from Methodist to Apostolic; from Presbyterian to Episcopalian; from Catholic to non-denominational; from conservative to liberal and from traditional to contemporary. Worship styles are as varied as a Brazilian smorgasbord!

It is unpopular for any believer to critique or question the black church in public. This is especially true if you are a black preacher. I am both, but I believe this is what actually gives me the credentials to confront, critique and to compliment the church.

IT'S IN MY BLOOD!

I was born and raised in the black church; in fact, in the very one I pastor at the time of this writing. I confessed having received the Divine Call and delivered my first sermon at age 15 to a packed house of family and friends. At age 18, two months after my high school graduation, I was called by our congregation of about 150 to become their pastor. At the time I was the youngest pastor in Texas. Today, our church has 5,000 members and anchors a 50-plus acre development which includes a park, a retail plaza which is the home of multiple small businesses, television production facility, two schools, an apartment complex and two middle class subdivisions.

Every generation prior to mine on both my mother's and father's side of the family provided service and leadership in the church. My maternal roots are grounded in the Church of God in Christ (COGIC), founded by Bishop Charles H. Mason. Whenever he visited Houston, Bishop Mason lodged with my relatives. My great-grandmother, Ida Duncan Barnes, was a missionary as were her daughters Lou Ivory Littlejohn and Jesse Galloway. Hotels were not open to blacks in those days. My maternal grandmother, Victoria Turner Barnes, held several offices in that denomination including President of Business and Professional Women's Federation and member of the National Board of Trustees.

Paternally, my family's foundation is Baptist. My great grand-father founded two churches over a century ago: the Antioch Baptist Church in Henderson, Texas and the Antioch Baptist Church in Duncan, Oklahoma. My father's dad, Rev. C. D. Dixon, pastored the Mt. Pillow Baptist Church, our home church, which is now The Community Of Faith, for fifty years (1928-1978). My siblings and I were born and raised in this church by our parents, James and Carrol Dixon, Sr., who remain active and devoted churchmen to this day.

It's in my blood! The [black] church has been my life. I have served as choir director, Sunday School teacher, auxiliary president, associate minister and now have been a pastor for 25 years.

I must hasten to add that this is not a *"me vs. them"* discourse. The black church is too much of who I am and I am too much of what it is. Whatever it is or is not, I have in some way contributed to this reality. I share in its glory as well as its grief. So in many ways, this is a self critique because the black church is in me.

It is my conviction that in many aspects, this institution is most responsible for the good we have come to experience in this nation. Yet, on the other hand, through negligence, it has contributed to the reasons blacks are doing so bad. In my view, the black church has the burden of leading our community to make a turn-around and once again create a new wave of progress in black America.

A UNIQUE BLACK MESSAGE

Through the black church a unique theology was produced— "liberation theology." This is the interpretation of God as the Omnipresent Sovereign who is interested in and committed to the progressive liberation of the devalued, disenfranchised victims of oppressive systems. This theology gave us, and the broader world, a view of God as One who loves those subjected to evil and the One who empowers the oppressed to endure and overcome undeserved injustice.

It is through our distinctive interpretation of the Old Testament drama which features God's chosen people, Israel, and their deliverance from slavery after 400 years, that liberation theology derives. The Egyptians were their oppressors; Moses was their emancipator who led them across the Red Sea into a newly discovered freedom. God's power was greatly displayed on behalf of the physically inferior group as they overcame the military superiority of Pharaoh's army. The parallelism of Israel's experience and the black experience gave rise to this empowering view of God, ourselves, our plight and our future. This theology provided a basis for our dignity, self-respect and our expectation of eventual justice for which we trust God to bring about.

This is a brand of theology that no other group in America could have produced because it was formed in the crucible of the singular experience of the Negro in America. Only a people whose plight had been similar to the enslaved Israelites could feel the agony of their dilemma. Only those who had suffered a similar degradation and humiliation could relate to the magnitude of emancipation's meaning.

THE JOSHUA GENERATION

Only through the unique perspective of colored people who had been disenfranchised and marginalized, could one identify with the nomadic encounters of the Israelites in their post-slavery era. For truly the wilderness wandering for the Israelites was a period of instability and uncertainty.

Blacks were motivated to maintain hope through their interpretation of the biblical account of the Joshua generation who eventually made it to the Promise Land. Black liberation theology had its roots firmly planted in the soil of this Old Testament saga. The fruit of which was a generation of liberating leaders who organized and mobilized the masses to participate in their own deliverance. Chief among these was Dr. Martin Luther King, Jr. James Cone, in his book, *Malcolm and Martin in America: A Dream or A Nightmare,* reminds us of the following, "They [Negroes] did not have to be convinced of the inhumanity of segregation. All Negroes whether rich or poor, the ones who graduated from 'Morehouse or No house,' as King often said, knew from personal experience what it meant to be insulted, kicked in the seat of their pants, and spat upon by white people. What they needed was to be inspired and taught the most effective way, morally and practically to fight for justice."

Black liberation theology helped King and others to frame their message and their methods for leading black people to bear the responsibility to change their own predicament aided by God's power.

We also learned through this theology how God works through human agency—more explicitly through chosen and anointed leaders, to rescue, restore and relocate His people. This is why Negro leaders who placed themselves in harm's way for the sake of liberating and inspiring our people have always been compared to Moses and Joshua. Personalities like Harriet Tubman, Marcus Garvey, Sojourner Truth, Dr. Martin Luther King, Jr., and others have been assigned these titles in respect to their significant roles. They lived sacrificially for our collective empowerment.

It is not coincidental that the most influential figures in black life have primarily been preachers and others tied to the church. This fact is seen in past history and in the contemporary moment. We derived from the uniqueness of black liberation theology an understanding that there is sense to our struggle, meaning to our misery and purpose for our pain.

OUR IDENTITY

At a time when the African American community is in its most vulnerable state since the turn of the last century, it seems our church is more detached than ever from our reality. I have observed: *Our conversation is not about our crisis. Our message is not about our misery. Our ministries do not support a collective movement. Our power is not used for our progress.*

Before any critique can be communicated, there must be an acknowledgment of the positive things the black church has done and continues to do, something which is too seldom noted.

Historically, the church has been the single most influential organization in the progress of our race. It has been the bastion of human rights, the impetus for education, the engine for economic empowerment and the catalyst for political and social reform. It has produced and provided our most prolific voices of anointed advocacy. It has also been an embracing family, an encouraging community and our most effective social services agency.

The black church has been our foremost source of information and inspiration. Being the only place for so long where blacks could gather and control the agenda, the church provided more than a house for spiritual encounters. Additionally, it provided a forum for resourceful and relevant discussion. The ongoing conversations concerning the plight of the ex-slave community who were learning what it meant to be free and how to become and function as a freed people, took place in the black church. This is where prayers were prayed, goals were set, strategies were planned and where courage and faith to fight were inspired. It is also where the cause of freedom was confirmed to be a righteous pursuit and where the strength to love those who oppressed us was taught.

"BATTLESHIP" CHURCHES

In the black church, congregations became armies; soldiers were led by pastors who were generals and captains. They understood the church's pivotal role in inspiring and giving power to our race.

These churches were battleships and they came to the rescue whenever blacks and others were under siege. Battleship churches moved to the front line for our defense and deliverance. They were a force to be reckoned with by anyone or anything that threatened to prevent us from overcoming. These churches worked in education, economics and politics, using their spiritual and numerical strength to challenge the system. They also challenged blacks to accept responsibility for participating in our own uplift.

In the latter part of the 20th century something happened. A transition occurred that almost went unnoticed and very few people have been willing to tell it like it is. Some are too cowardly, others are caught on the wrong side of the equation, and still others simply are not aware of the problem.

In command of our battleships, pastors were warriors who knew how to watch, fight and pray. They were the independent voices in the black community. As a result, they could lead in the fight for justice and equality. The black church was where we were trained, challenged and motivated to be vigilant about education, political involvement and other self-enabling activities.

There we learned moral values, and personal and social responsibility. The family, church and educational institutions were intertwined in a progressive partnership. Yet, they relied on the church to provide spiritual and moral guidance.

Schools counted on concerned parents to send them students who had basic home training, a moral foundation, knowing right from wrong, discipline and manners. Schools were expected to provide quality education. Teachers were looked to as role models who displayed moral character, dignity, and class. This was a winning partnership in which the church set the standard and influenced every facet of our community. When this paradigm prevailed the black community was nearly viable and unstoppable. Our collective progress was more than steady.

THE CRUISE SHIP EMERGES!

Today, this prototype is nearly non-existent. The lead entity, the black church, has transitioned from battleship to cruise ship. This is where a profound change occurred—and there are distinct differences. Cruise ships sail for the purpose of fun and relaxation and are only interested in calm and tranquil seas. They work hard at being comfortable rather than powerful. They invest more in looking good than they do in doing good work. People who board (join) cruise ship churches expect a vacation rather than a vocation. The captain and crew are skilled at customer service but not at training soldiers and anointed warriors. Battleships, on the other hand, understand convenience is not the priority. They are acutely aware that we have territory to conquer and adversaries to confront.

PROFILING THE CRUSE SHIP

Cruise ships are led by entertainment specialists who are skilled at guiding ships while keeping their passengers (customers) peaceful, happy, and excited. Rough waters and confrontation are to be avoided at all cost. They will never intentionally show up where a battle on behalf of blacks or others needs to be fought. For example:

- They would never challenge corporate America on its inequitable procurement policies and the exportation of jobs which leads to the erosion of a sacrificed middle class.
- They would never openly challenge the government's response to Hurricane Katrina or question the poorly constructed levies.
- They did not show up when James Byrd, Jr. was dragged to death in Jasper, Texas by racists.
- They do not challenge the states and school districts on the matter of inequitable school funding and race-biased testing.
- They do not question or challenge government budgets and policies that perpetuate poverty and disenfranchisement of minorities and the poor.
- They do not publicly hold blacks accountable who jeopardize the future of the race by insidious, immoral and illegal behavior.
- They do not participate in collective efforts to turn the black community into a powerful force.
- They do not accept responsibility for screening politicians to ensure they are worthy of representing the black community's interest.

Recently, a coalition was formed in our city called Houston Coalition of Working People and the Poor. It's purpose is to unite churches, community based organizations, labor unions, elected officials, and others who embraced the need to advocate on behalf of working people and poor people who are negatively impacted by adverse public policies. One of our first efforts was to address the need to increase the minimum wage. Another was to deal with the fact that nearly 40 million Americans are without healthcare. One would think every church, especially black churches, would enthusiastically join such a coalition. To the contrary, we found it amazingly difficult to inspire pastors and churches to get involved. Perhaps they were out on a cruise!

There is so much evil in the world and so much working against African Americans that to be disengaged with the real war is unexplainable and unacceptable. The nature of light is to attack darkness—it is aggressive. Cruise ships, however, are passive. This explains why they are essentially non-confrontational. Although some cruise ships represent themselves to be Afro-centric, meaning they emphasize cultural awareness and appreciation, they often do not engage in the economic, educational, political, and other dilemmas that threaten our community. They may even wear indigenous garb during February, but they will not overtly challenge poisonous policies or the paralyzing practices which continue to undermine our progress.

WHERE IS THE CONCERN?

Cruise ships help to reinforce the ME ONLY philosophy of this self-centered culture. Messages in these churches almost totally focus on personal prosperity, personal success and individual achievement. Cruise ship ministers choose to avoid challenging their congregations concerning collective commitment to the elevation of the group. Frankly, that message is disturbing and disrupting to the ME ONLY mindsets of the passengers—who desire to sail in a different direction. The battle many African Americans have with poverty, poor health, illiteracy and criminality is not the concern of the cruise ship congregations. Our quest for economic improvement is also not a conversation that excites them because they are independently comfortable.

Cruise ship churches are typically middle class environments which qualify as mega churches because of their size, (3,000 or more members). Many are super mega, having 10,000-plus members. These congregations are affluent, highly visible and extremely attractive. Everything is slick, polished, professionally packaged and presented. All of this is to the credit of pastors and church leaders, who are impressively intelligent and concretely committed to excellence, which is a good thing. All churches should be. Unfortunately, the resourcefulness of the mega cruise ships seldom impacts the crippling conditions, common to the black community. Let me pose a few serious questions:

- When there is a crisis in your city, who are the black pastors and churches you expect to see and hear addressing the problem?
- When there has been an injustice committed in your community, who were the pastors that stepped forward and spoke up on behalf of justice?
- What churches in your city are working to correct problems of illiteracy, poverty, housing and healthcare deficiency among blacks and others who are economically and politically disenfranchised?
- Is there a pastor or a group of pastors in your area who are spreading the message about our collective empowerment?

Again, these are not cruise ship concerns and the pastors of this brand of church do not identify with these issues through proclamation or participation. Why not?

INSULATED FROM THE PAIN

Cruise ship churches are the fastest growing congregations in the country. It is phenomenal to see their swift growth. Their ministry philosophy obviously appeals to 21st century mentality and the messages are speaking to their passenger's number one interest: SELF! "How can I prosper? How can I be rich? How can I have the dream relationship? How can I be happy?"—are their driving themes. This message is not innately wrong, but if not balanced with commitment to the entire group, it is immeasurably harmful. Consequently, the comfortable cushions are filled. People are coming by the thousands and dollars by the millions, which for many define ultimate success. One cannot argue with the results from a business perspective. But, Luke 4:18 and Matthew 25 may challenge us to think differently.

Pastors, or cruise ship directors, are normally well compensated and are forever delivered from the pain of poverty and personal subjection to the reality of the black masses and others who are disadvantaged. Therefore, they are insulated from the stresses of most blacks and are tempted to no longer contemplate the prevailing condition. Of course, failure to consider this results in messages and ministries which do not relate to their reality. Cruise ship pastors strategically avoid upsetting the atmosphere on the boat with news of crime, double-digit unemployment, generational decadence, closing of black schools, systematic injustice, dilapidated neighborhoods and the nullification of civil rights gains by conservative courts.

Because of these and other prevailing issues, this is a season for battleships. Only churches that are directed by warriors and staffed with soldiers will be found where the real war is being waged. The strongholds the adversary has on blacks are not at all inconspicuous. They are clearly evident and those who are suffering understand this well. The problem is, too few churches are prepared to take the issues on. Only battleships work here. Cruise ships cannot and will not respond.

First, they have a problem with personnel. The captain and crew are not soldiers. Fighting is not their forte.

Second, their passengers are not sailors or soldiers. They are success and serenity seekers who are attracted by the celebrity status of their leader. They do not respect him because of battles he has won, but they admire him because of blessings he displays. Soldiers respect leaders who have battle scars, having obtained their spoils through combat.

Third, the psychological orientation of a cruise ship passenger is not suited for battleships. On a battleship all the passengers are members of the crew. They are knowingly on board to share the responsibilities for operating the ship, making sure the vessel is battle ready, and are expecting conflict. Cruise ship passengers pay the fare to vacate responsibility and to escape any problems associated with their reality.

What is Your Answer?

Do you think we need battleships when:

- 68% of new HIV/AIDS cases are African American females?
  ☐ Yes   ☐ No
- More black males are going to prison than college?
  ☐ Yes   ☐ No
- Two generations of blacks are more proficient in street language than English language?
  ☐ Yes   ☐ No
- There are only 30 black owned banks in the entire U.S.?
  ☐ Yes   ☐ No
- Blacks control so little of the hotel and restaurant industry?
  ☐ Yes   ☐ No
- Blacks have little to no control in the energy industry?
  ☐ Yes   ☐ No
- This country can spend $100 billion a year fighting a war in Iraq—whether you are for or against it—but our schools and after school programs are grossly under-funded?
  ☐ Yes   ☐ No
- So many working people remain poor and without health insurance?
  ☐ Yes   ☐ No
- The minimum wage is not close to a living wage?
  ☐ Yes   ☐ No
- One million black men are in prison?
  ☐ Yes   ☐ No

With conditions like these, why isn't every black pastor and church speaking out and doing something concerning the situation? Cruise ship pastors are content to sail on smooth seas, assuring the passengers everything is fine. They choose not to warn of the impending dangers that are lurking. Others are so overwhelmed by the magnitude of our crisis they attempt to drown out reality with noise about superficial victories. Still there are others in leadership who are grossly uninformed about our plight. They are reading the wrong books, idolizing the wrong preachers and emulating cruise ship models.

BATTLESHIPS TO THE FOREFRONT!

Obviously, this is a season for battleship ministries. Our history proves that when we were faced with formidable opposition, it was battleships led by ministers who were warriors God used to advance our united cause. Even those who did not participate in the war were beneficiaries of the gains.

Admittedly, operating a battleship is becoming increasingly difficult in this cruise ship era. The pastor who dares to run his church like a warship does so at great risk because such a large percentage of today's populous is only receptive to luxury liner environments. There are not many who will volunteer to go to war. Thus, while the crisis of our times calls for military-like ministry, it is unpopular to proclaim this message. But believe me, if the black community does not wake up from this state of mental lethargy and prepare to join and support battleship churches, we will find ourselves without a voice to speak for us, a vehicle to deliver us, and no victories to celebrate.

A NEW THEOLOGY

In this century, the black church must resurrect a new version of a unique theology. The former version was rightfully labeled "liberation theology." The new version should be labeled "empowerment theology." This fresh message must explain our history, define our identity, and clarify our destiny.

Tragically, most African Americans remain unfamiliar with our history and therefore, disconnected from our legacy. This impedes the possibility of discovering our true identity. The self perception of blacks in this generation is damaged and devoid of a sacred sense of self. As a result, there are growing numbers of African Americans who have disdain and disregard for what it means to be black.

First, there are those who debase our blackness by being intentionally slouchy and blatantly indecent. Exposing one's underwear to the public is an example. By the way, underwear is to

147

be worn under your clothes!

Second, there are others who devalue blackness by their determination to remain unlearned and unskilled. This too is a gross misrepresentation of our collective blackness.

Third, there are those who disdain blackness by their unwillingness to be identified with anything that is significantly black. This includes black churches, schools, neighborhoods, organizations and causes. Such individuals view themselves to be, in the words of Michael Eric Dyson, "incidentally black." In their minds their blackness is not something to be taken seriously by themselves or others. It is a fact they actually try to forget.

A true empowerment theology that is grounded and rooted in scripture would give divine legitimacy and validity to our blackness. It would reveal we are a peculiar people of noble purpose among our fellow man. It would demand values-based character and socially responsible behavior which lifts the race and contributes to the holistic progression of humanity.

This theology would explain that blacks, too, are created in the image and likeness of God—fearfully and wonderfully made. Being black is a beautiful thing. Therefore, our blackness is a spectacular blessing, not a damning curse. The immense degree of inferiority which continues to plague African Americans is made possible through the absence of this understanding. The black church has not preached this message, therefore, this new generation has not heard it. Because they have not heard it, they have not believed it; neither do they live it.

We are also endowed with the right and responsibility of exercising a degree of dominion in the earth. This is the Genesis mandate. Armed with this message, blacks would be motivated to learn and put into practice principles of capitalism. We would understand the connection between building wealth in our community and fulfilling our commitment to serving God. I call this concept, Kingdom Capitalism, which means amassing wealth through God-honoring methodologies which blesses others and preserves the environment.

TAKING TERRITORY

To a large degree, blacks continue to suffer with low expectations. We don't anticipate ever exercising real power and authority in the world. Unfortunately, many blacks and others have falsely concluded that we are forever relegated to the margins. Empowerment theology would address this gross error in judgment. Without it there is little reason for blacks to hope for more than survival. As Carter G. Woodson explained in *The Mis-Education of the Negro*, "Our great sin is low aim."

This new brand of empowerment theology must encourage blacks to aim high, to prepare ourselves intellectually and financially, to control the flow of wealth for generations. It would teach us the difference between being rich and being wealthy. Businessman Michael V. Roberts explains that it is time for us to learn the distinction between the two. According to Roberts, "Being rich gives you power, but being wealthy gives you authority." In a recent conversation with him, he stated, "Being rich makes a person or a family comfortable during one lifetime, but being wealthy empowers generations." Let me encourage you to read his book, *Action Has No Season.*

I am convinced there is an urgent need for blacks to be inspired to use their faith, godly wisdom and education to advance in significant markets. We cannot sit on the sidelines for another decade or two watching the economic explosion that's taking place globally. We need to get in the game and we must play to win. This is what the "now" generation holds against the previous generation. It appears that we failed to take advantage of opportunities to truly strengthen and enable our race through amassing wealth.

Take time to read Claud Anderson's book, *PowerNomics*. More than inspiring, it is also insightful as to the historic role of the black church as an economic institution and what the potential of black America is should the church rise to meet the challenges and opportunities of today.

The Promise Land vision was more than about changing addresses; it was about changing status. The land in Canaan was fertile and productive. Capturing and conquering this territory positioned the Israelites to have authority over markets and control the flow of wealth in the region. This is the model the new version of empowerment theology must present and blacks must embrace. Our goals cannot simply be to get *an* education and get *a* job and buy *a* house and purchase *a* car. This again is low aim. We must begin to envision our race controlling the real estate market, controlling the creation of jobs, controlling a significant segment of the auto industry, not just buying gasoline, but producing and distributing energy resources.

Be mindful, however, that the Promise Land was not handed to the Israelites on a social welfare platter. It was not the result of the good will of the Canaanites, who were under the conviction that the Israelites had experienced a hard time and deserved a break and a blessing. On the contrary, God told His new Commander in Chief, Joshua the preacher, you are to lead My people to Canaan to *take* the land I swore to give them. Every piece of ground they gained was secured through battle. The fact is, we are well able to go up and possess the land, capture the markets and control a respectful percentage of the nations and the world's wealth, but we must do it collectively, strategically and worshipfully.

A VOICE OF EMPOWERMENT

The black church must commit to being the voice of empowerment and enlightenment which is necessary to re-educate, re-orientate and motivate African Americans to realign ourselves with our God-given identity and our purposed destiny. This is our calling—to speak life into our people. The voice of our church must once again become clearly distinguishable from others because we are speaking to people in a peculiar predicament.

The new version of empowerment theology must be authentic. To be so, it must posses the same DNA (deoxyribonucleic acid) as the theology of James Cone, Howard Thurman, Otis Moss, Gardner Taylor, Martin Luther King, Jr. and others who helped to shape it. The new version must have roots which run deep into our history so that it is nurtured by the faith of our fathers and becomes a continuum of their vision that "we shall overcome."

However, there's a special caveat to this new brand of theological thought. It must be Afro-centric but not Afro-singular. It must serve to consolidate the resourcefulness of blacks while remaining open to the formulation of strategic alliances with potential partners of other races and cultures. Remember, this is a global economy, which should not intimidate us because our Father has the whole world in His hands. With amplified volume, the black pastor and church must speak truth to power. Not only must we educate people concerning the possibilities based on the promises of God, we must also teach them concerning the process by which the possibilities become realities. We must steer away from the brand of prosperity gospel which does not include factual process, but only promotes naming and claiming it, a belief that conditions people to have false hopes and to *wait for* what has to be *worked for.*

The church must biblically validate our right and responsibility to cultivate wealth. We must begin at early childhood levels to instill the principles associated with power and authority in our children. Each new generation has to know there is a godly and honorable way to live securely. They must also understand that each generation has the responsibility of leaving a legacy of spiritual, familial, intellectual and material wealth.

KEEP THE FAITH

Wake up sleeping giant! We have the power to save our community. Our message, when based in the liberating theology of scripture, is one that will reinstate the values and principles sufficient to ground and guide us to nobler heights. Once more, we need visionary ministries to take the lead and fuel our movement toward the promised place, uniting our people in this common pursuit. We must again inspire our people with faith to believe that our destiny may have been delayed, but cannot and will not be denied.

CHAPTER EIGHT

WE ARE DIVIDED AND FALLING

We need a vision to unite and ignite us.

The occasion was my 20th Pastoral Anniversary Gala. I was 39 years of age and leaders within our congregation determined that an elaborate celebration was much deserved. An impressive crowd gathered at the Wortham Center in downtown Houston and it was a sold out event.

Some were a bit surprised when they learned of my choice for the keynote speaker's slot. A few members of the committee expected I would have selected one of the young or at least middle-age mega-church leader types whose popularity would have helped to sell tickets and would readily appeal to many of the young professionals who would be in attendance.

My choice was the sage, the late Dr. E.V. Hill who was then pastor of Mt. Zion Baptist Church in Los Angeles, California. I wanted a person who had impacted my life profoundly and whose ministry had enlightened and empowered people globally. I wanted an individual who was proud to be black and had built meaningful relationships trans-racially—someone who had been black Baptist traditionally, who was not bound denominationally. That person had to be the one of a kind, Edward Victor Hill.

Two Troubling Questions

Due to a lengthy illness, Pastor Hill was physically feeble, not his vibrant, robust self as in days past. Actually, he spoke while sitting on a stool. He began by explaining why he was determined to be there in spite of his obvious discomfort. His explanation humbled me even more, and then he proceeded to speak to the sensitized audience in a grandfatherly tone. His speech was absolutely classic and the moment was nothing short of historic.

In this chapter, I hope to transmit the pain that I heard in Dr. Hill's voice which he sought to convey to us. His was the pain of a father nearing departure from his family, dealing with their state of decline. He saw us as divided, with no inspired direction or vision.

The venerable Dr. Hill posed two most penetrating questions which riveted the audience to their seats and sent each mind on a course of introspection. I share them with you as I have with countless groups across the country and with scores of persons in casual conversation.

The first question he raised was, "Will this generation of Negroes or African Americans, as you prefer to be called, ever become a people again?" The second question was as convicting as the first. It is: "Will this generation of African Americans, new Negroes, prove to have what it takes to make leaders among us great?"

It must be extremely disturbing and somewhat depressing for those who prayed, marched, fought, endured insult, sacrificed and stood against the tide to move us forward, to face twilight, knowing our vulnerable circumstance. This was "Papa" Hill's burden—even heavier than his physical malady. He wanted to die with affirmative answers to these two questions, yet not quite having the assurance troubled his soul.

From the moment I heard them, these questions have lived with me and I with them. Hopefully, they will take up permanent residence in your heart and you will be motivated to be a part of the positive answer.

This senior leader of the church and elder of the black family was there to challenge a generation who are heirs of a rich legacy.

Apparently, he was troubled in spirit concerning the reality he discerned and described to us in quite clear terms. He exposed the two contrasting mentalities that distinguished blacks of a former era from those at the turn of this century. He was bothered by the fact this generation of African Americans are consumed with a ME mentality which is distinctly and disturbingly different from the WE mentality which formerly characterized blacks when we were called Negroes and Coloreds.

"WE" VERSUS "ME"

It is important for us to know the difference between the two mentalities. When we operated as WE, there was evidence of our collective potency and productivity. When the WE mentality prevailed:

- We built schools and universities
- We founded social justice organizations
- We educated our children, instilling in them the goal of being twice as good because we were aware that the world was unfair
- We started businesses and created wealth within our community
- We shared a stick of butter and a cup of flour with our neighbors
- We raised our children as an entire village
- We secured the right to vote and did so in large numbers.

Now African Americans who epitomize the ME mentality have quite a different record and reputation. We are overtly self-centered and unapologetically disconnected. Consider these results of the ME mentality:

- We lost schools and universities
- Our social justice organizations struggle to survive
- Our dropout rate is soaring and illiteracy handicaps our people as a whole

- We have few black owned businesses
- We do not typically know our neighbors and dare not think of asking for a morsel of bread or a cup of milk

The accomplishments of blacks who possess the WE mentality prove what can be expected when we work together as a people group. In other words, comprehending the WE mindset is fundamental to understanding the prior progress of a people, who were bombarded by countless disadvantages. There were so many barriers constructed to prevent blacks from ever becoming a full, an educated and economically viable people. There were philosophical ideologies, antagonistic public policies and polluted perceptions to overcome. These were evils that could not be confronted by a people who were divided and unsure of direction. It took blacks and members of other races uniting on the basis of common core beliefs; one of which is that all men are indeed created equal and are endowed with certain inalienable rights; among which are life, liberty and the pursuit of happiness. In spite of these formidable enforcers of oppression, things changed.

While advancement has definitely been made, this progress is now in jeopardy. This advance is only attributed to a group of people for whom any other reality was unacceptable. They were united by circumstance and conviction, in principle and in practice. They realized that what they had in common was far more significant than the things which were not. Thus, when they referred to one another as brothers and sisters, they meant it. These are terms which today are seldom used and when they are, they are merely symbolic.

DIVIDED ON EVERY SIDE

The fact blacks are divided, meaning we are not thinking and acting as a people, has been sufficiently proven. It is a reality lamented by many African Americans and blacks who recognize in multiple contexts how this cripples us. Everywhere you look, in each category you examine, you will discover how divided we are.

Our churches are divided by denomination, by convention, by

philosophy, by size and economic strength. It is difficult to think of any one thing we could not do if we work together. In 2005, four black Baptist Conventions met at a joint session in Nashville, Tennessee. According to Dr. Melvin Wade, past president of National Missionary Baptist Convention, it was a positive encounter. It began a healing and bonding process that was long overdue. Unity was the theme. A front page of the Tennessean Newspaper dated January 26, 2005 read, *"Unity is the byword at Baptist conclave."*

The good news is, a second joint gathering is being planned. Wouldn't it be awesome if the groups found common ground and merged. An organization that powerful could do wonders for our community.

Our social justice organizations are not as unified as they could and should be. While they at least come together at a time of crisis, I do not know that there has been a recent summit of social justice organizations to craft an agenda. There should be an understanding of which organization is doing what and how the consolidated strengths of all are brought to bear on addressing certain issues. Instead, our social justice groups have sought to carve out individual turf and make names for themselves apart from one another. The best example of this is the relationship between Jesse Jackson, Rainbow PUSH and Al Sharpton, National Action Network. Although they can't possibly always agree, they share insights, influence and resourcefulness with each other.

Black elected officials are too often divided on the issues, and this is to be expected. But it seems when it comes to dealing with problems facing black people, there could be a consensus reached on what the priorities are and an agreement on how to address them. There are too many stories of blacks making deals independently which undermine the agreed on objectives and strategies of the group. I am certainly not advocating that African American elected persons should only focus on black issues. Of course, they are obligated to serve their total constituencies with quality. However, the perspective and passion they are uniquely positioned to bring to bear on matters related to our community are necessary. I know of counties in which black elected officials never meet as a group, not even annually, do not talk and actually work to destroy each other's influence. This is sad and our community cannot afford such division. We need to ask, what is the seven year agenda for black political forces at every level?

NEEDED: INTELLECTUAL CAPITAL

Blacks in education are divided. This is a travesty in view of the present trend of African American youth. In nearly every state in the union, the number of black males incarcerated is greater than those receiving college educations. I also remind you that the academic achievement gap is not closing, but widening. Additionally, there is the problem that blacks are being systematically weeded out of governmental and administrative positions. The fact so few young African Americans in general, and men in particular, consider education as a meaningful career option is alarming. These are only some of the reasons blacks in education need not be divided. The future of our race depends on our intellectual capital.

We are also separated economically and this too is critical. There is no arguing that our economic evolution is stymied and something must be done to change it. We still do not have an agenda we can unite to implement. Be sure, we have no shortage of economic thinkers who have made substantive suggestions for us to consider. But what we do not have is a widely accepted, economic empowerment council who meets to collaborate and set forth an agenda agreed on by consensus. Such discussions should address questions like...

- How we can save and rebuild historically black neighborhoods.
- How we can infiltrate industries wherein blacks have been historically forbidden or marginalized.

I agree with Jesse Jackson that one such industry is the energy sector. I live in Houston, the energy capital, and blacks have very little to do with it, other than consuming oil and gas. Additional industries would include banking and finance, hotels and restaurants, sports and entertainment—beyond performing to owning. There are others for sure, but we need a plan developed by our leading economic thinkers.

These are only examples of the consequences of not thinking and acting as a people. None of these crucial, life and death matters are being appropriately dealt with because we are cursing ourselves through the ME mentality and have not been willing to make leaders among us great. This is not God's fault. It is ours!

VISION COMES FIRST

Dr. Robert Schuller, "Mr. Possibility" himself, shared a great piece of wisdom on this point. He says whenever he had a vision, it was always beyond his available resources. Thus, the process of deciding whether or not to do it went something like...

1. Will it honor God?
2. Will it bless people?
3. Is it really needed?
4. Does it require faith?

Schuller says he has never started with the question, "How much will it cost?"—and the number-crunching bean counters were not brought in until they had decided they were going to commit to a particular vision. Why? Because a big vision always costs big dollars and big money discussed upfront will drown out the dream. This is the kind of faith and the type of visionary I admire. With God's help, I have operated the same way much of my career. Is it a mistake free system? Of course not. But more often than not, it is a winning formula and it's the stuff greatness is made of.

My definition of vision is, *"A divinely inspired portrait of possibility, fueled by God's power to accomplish God's purpose, through God's people for God's praise."*

EMPOWERMENT VILLAGES

One of the conspicuously missing ingredients in black America which is necessary for any ethnic culture to thrive, and certainly to succeed, is geographically identifiable zones/districts that facilitate social and economic transactions. Every culture must have commercial centers to which they are committed and that hopefully attract others to do business. We had them when segregation made it necessary. We supported our business districts because we lacked access to others. Outside our community, this is a positive characteristic of other ethnic cultures in our nation who have made great progress as people groups. They have planned and done strategically, what we did only by necessity.

Think of Asians, and how in most urban cities there are areas that flourish with a business and residential mix, populated by Chinese, Koreans or Vietnamese. Similar developments established by Latinos and Middle Easterners also are common. These districts display and re-enforce cultural pride and are profitable as well.

This is not to suggest we will ever be able to do 100% of our business with blacks. That is completely unrealistic and is an unhealthy concept. We will always have a need to trade with and partner with other races and cultures; not only locally, but globally. Chinatown is not off limits to non-Chinese. The Galleria Mall in Houston is not restricted to whites or Jews. And I know where to go when I am hungry for real Indian or Middle Eastern cuisine!

What African Americans lack is an empowered presence. When I say this, I mean a respected presence that is based on economic stability within a defined cultural context. Please remember, respect in the true sense is always earned and never given. Thus, in the 21st century, blacks have to be determined to earn the respect we want from each other, whites, and other cultures. We cannot expect or demand it simply because we are black. By claiming and developing territory we can position ourselves as a self-sufficient force that is not at the mercy of market trends controlled by others. God bless the child who has his own!

Currently, we are not respected. Other races cannot say this publicly, but it is true. More and more we are dismissed and dissed by people who understand power. This is because we have no commitment to united self-sufficiency. Everywhere we go, everything we do, everything we buy, all supports someone else's power base. This is why it is so easy to disrespect us.

To earn the esteem we desire will require, among many things, building our own bases of economic and community empowerment. I deliberately placed economic empowerment in front of community empowerment because economics is the blood that must be in circulation for any community to survive and grow.

We need a vision and strategic plan for creating Black Empowerment Districts (Villages) in every major city in America. These districts should become economic engines which grow existing entrepreneurs, create new entrepreneurs, redevelop and resurrect run-down sections of our communities that once thrived. Moreover, it will create a powerful presence which will inspire our culture, especially our youth, to believe in themselves and to truly be proud of who we are as a people.

What does this mean? Let me ask you to repeat this declaration: ***"We are going where we have never gone; to do what we have never done; to have what we have never had and to become who we are purposed to be."***

"Can it really happen?" you ask. "Can we (blacks) really get it together?" The answer is an empathic, optimistic, visionary, YES!

VISIONARIES ARE NEEDED

This is a vision that should include community development corporations, local banks, municipalities, HUD, business chambers and other strategic partners. There would be little need for creating new entities because most of what is required already exists. The problem is, these organizations are functioning as disconnected parts. This is why our success remains personal and impact remains marginal. But when our leadership agrees to embrace something more inclusive, the results will be generational and phenomenal. Again, a common vision is the basis for unity.

I pray you agree it is time for a movement which is bigger, more consequential and revolutionary.

WE'RE LOSING GROUND—LITERALLY

It would be foolish to act as though we do not recognize what is occurring around the country. In Houston, Texas, we see what is happening. Historically black neighborhoods that were deserted, not only by the black middle class but also by the working class, are no longer ours. Real estate developers are making major moves and major money.

After years of intentional neglect by local government, people with any means moved out, due to inner city blight. Left behind were mostly the elderly, some renters and a few landowners. Now whites, who took flight first are rapidly returning to redeveloped urban centers. Blacks chased them to the suburbs, now they are returning to the most valuable land reclaiming their political base and saving fuel.

This is not pure coincidence. Urban planning discussions take place to which we are not privy; this has happened for years. Hopefully, we will begin to have the same kind of diligence and designs for the future of our communities. The fact is, if we do not develop a plan that makes sense for us, we will continue to be subjected to those that are not made with us in mind. In an earlier chapter, I mentioned Freedmen's Town, an area in Houston that had been carved out as a niche for ex-slaves at the turn of the 19th century. It no longer exists. Today, it is called Mid Town and features lofts, condominiums and town homes ranging from $300,000 to $1 million. Blacks did not plan for this to happen, neither did we plan for it *not* to.

CONNECTING THE PIECES

When our academic, business, church, economic and political minds unite in a partnership around a vision to energize our communities, what are the limits? There are none!

It would be worth a trip to look at the signature work of Dr. Floyd Flake, Greater Allen Cathedral and the Allen Neighborhood Preservation and Development Corporation. They have essentially created a model every city needs, and they have done it on a grand scale. While you are in New York, you should check out the work of Dr. Johnny Youngblood at St. Paul Community Baptist Church and St. Paul Economic Development Corporation. The housing program called the Nehemiah Project is phenomenal. Over 2,000 single family detached units have been built and sold. And of course, in Houston, I am proud of my colleagues, Pastor Kirbyjon Caldwell at Windsor Village UMC and the Pyramid CDC; a visit to their Power Center and Corinthian Point subdivision would convince you too. Then there's Pastor Harvey Clemons of the Pleasant Hill Baptist Church and the Fifth Ward CDC. Their housing projects and retail development center are more than admirable. They are impressive. There is also Pastor William Lawson, Pastor Emeritus at Wheeler Avenue Baptist Church and the W.A. Lawson Institute for Peace and Prosperity (WALIPP). Their development work is also multifaceted and pacesetting.

Our work through The Community Of Faith Church and the Dominion Community Development Corporation is also comprehensive, including two subdivisions, Dominion Estates 1 & 2 and Dominion Square Apartments; Dominion Plaza Retail Center which is home to Dominion Academy Charter School and Dominion Park, a recreational facility.

There is not much we need to create. It is more a matter of connecting the powerful pieces which already exist. That is how we form what I call "collective potency." When you consider what is happening in our faith-based operations as well as in our private sector initiatives, our combined potential is unlimited. For example, check out the work churches are doing through community development corporations.

Then consider the outstanding work being done through private enterprise. Magic Johnson, proving that there is more to be done off the court than on, has set a great model through his commercial real estate development enterprise. The movie theaters, Starbucks, TGI Fridays and fitness centers he has invested in have not only been a success but have also provided a convincing model of what is possible. Sean "P Diddy" Combs has certainly set a great entrepreneurial example through his clothing line and other ventures. Master P has done well with his diverse investment endeavors. Oprah Winfrey has shown great commitment to addressing the needs of hurting people, particularly those living below the poverty line. Michael V. Roberts is another outstanding role model. He is a mogul in the hotel and commercial development sector. There are certainly many others who could be listed here. I heard Ms. Willie Barrows of Chicago say in a meeting, "We are not as much divided as we are disconnected." The point is, God has blessed us with the ingredients, but we have to be smart enough to mix them to create a masterpiece. Again, if we fail to do this, the fault is not with God.

LEADERSHIP MUST SURFACE

I really do believe that one day soon a group such as this could become the genesis of something truly revolutionary taking place in black America. What excuses will this generation of leaders have for not having done what is necessary to rescue our people from impending danger? We have the intellect, access to capital and competence, buying power and influence. And now, we have—the vision. Most importantly, God is on our side.

If those gifted to lead choose not to be involved, what excuse would there be 20 years from now when the thought of black Americans not reaching their potential is far more remote than now? Having to admit we gave up or we did not meet to plan the vision will be more than embarrassing. It would be so unlike those who came before us, who never stopped trying even though it meant dying.

Is this an invitation for your involvement? YES! More than that, it is a clarion call to lead at another dimension. We are not powerful because of the cars we drive, the houses we live in or where we take luxury vacations. Proverbs says, "A good man leaves an inheritance to his children's children." As a race, we have to think generationally. Fifty years from now, where will the evidence be that we were here and we lived for something beyond ourselves and our time. Empowerment Villages—it's a good place to start.

I see this as possible because I can embrace a vision which is bigger than myself. Plus, I believe there are hundreds of thousands who are willing to participate in, or simply waiting for, positive direction.

"SOMETHING SPECIAL"

Let me return to the Anniversary Gala and our guest, Dr. E.V. Hill.

The second question Dr. Hill raised deeply troubled me and continues to reverberate in my mind. He asked, "Will this generation of African Americans prove to have what it takes to make leaders great?"

Blacks everywhere should be challenged by this question.

Again, his tone was somber and you could hear the anguish of his soul in his voice. As Pappa Hill continued to expound on the statement couched in his question, one could deduce he had accepted the fact that his time left on this terrestrial ball was short. But he did not want to close his eyes with these issues unanswered or at least presented and considered.

What did he mean? He explained that one of the traits of former generations of blacks, when blacks were called Negroes, was their ability to identify a great leader before he became one. They could discern the spirit of a person who was destined to be great and had the ability to detect that "something special" in individuals living among them.

But this is only a part of it. The other aspect is that when they recognized the characteristics for group-empowering leadership in an individual, they had the ability and willingness to band together and make their leaders great. They knew how to support and strengthen the person's influence and how to cause others to respect them—which ultimately paid big dividends for the overall group.

Pappa Hill was disturbed because he had observed so much of the opposite with this new breed of blacks, called African Americans. We are apparently so consumed with our personal paths and pursuits that many of us do not have time to see what God has placed in other people for the benefit of all of us. We tend to lead such isolated and insulated lives that what is good for the group does not ever hit our radar screens. It surprises me to hear from African Americans who are not affiliated with any entity where black leadership is required—and who think it is an outdated concept.

In other words, many do not believe we need leadership, particularly group leaders, on any mass scale. They have become cynical towards anyone who is reputed to be a leader of the masses and are swift to detach from a person who is labeled a black leader.

Even more repudiating is when we do detect that "something special" in an individual which distinguishes them as a potential leader, then set out to prove the person is not special at all. Typically, we begin in denial, but after the leadership gifts and traits are totally obvious, we commence an all-out effort to destroy their chances before they ever get started.

A large percentage of our leadership are wounded or destroyed, not from frontal wounds, but from wounds inflicted from behind.

This is why Dr. Hill was so concerned. He had seen so many "could be great" black leaders undermined, betrayed and simply unsupported, leaving them damaged, defeated and discouraged. Others who could really help our collective cause, simply stay their distance because the price is too high, time is too short and our people are too vicious towards their own. We don't give white or other leaders anywhere near the hell we give our own. All of this is detrimental to our community and it has to change.

Dr. Hill was troubled that this generation lacked the gift of perception sufficient for recognizing unmanifested leadership potential in persons to whom we are familiar. So how is it done? It means being honest observers of people's capacity for influencing others, and formulating plans and strategies around an inspiring vision or purpose. It also takes having a knack for perceiving when an individual is grounded and driven toward an objective larger than they are. And certainly it means recognizing the kind of courage and bravado every leader must have in order to represent the needs of others in the face of opposition that such a vision naturally attracts.

Apparently, former generations had perceptibility, which enabled them to tap into a Harriet Tubman, Marcus Garvey, Sojourner Truth, Richard Allen and a Malcolm X.

Those who know the story of Rosa Parks, understand how she and her supporters saw that "special something" in the young pastor of Dexter Avenue Baptist Church, in Montgomery, Alabama, and drafted him to lead. His name? Martin Luther King, Jr. This is a graphic example of how being humanly selected is necessary for the fulfillment of the divine destiny of a race.

The ultimate fate of a people group is linked and inextricably tied to their ability to discern and willingness to draft into service those among them who are purposed to lead.

This is what makes the leadership question so important; it means life to our community. When people choose to ignore those who are destined to lead or fail to call, embrace, support and protect them, they seal their own negative fate; forfeiting their own futures.

SEEING POTENTIAL

Most in America would recognize the name Barbara Jordan, former member of the U.S. House of Representatives from Congressional District 18, in Houston. Her combined eloquence and intellect made her a powerful and productive force on behalf of all Americans—and particularly African Americans. But few would know the names of her childhood pastor and Sunday School teachers who saw in her an innate ability to command an audience and get her message across and who prepared and promoted her.

Most would not know the name of T.F. Freeman, the 50-plus-year coach of the Texas Southern University Debate team, who mentored a young teenage Barbara. He recalls vividly, "Barbara knew well how to talk when she arrived on campus, but I told her, 'I'm here to teach you how to think.'"

What Dr. Freeman saw in her was the potential to become something great for all of us. Our destinies were impacted because the people in her family, at the church and persons like Dr. Freeman perceived a great leader in the making was in their midst.

INCREASE THE INFLUENCE

Recognizing those who were purposed by the Creator to lead us into a new dimension is pivotal, but Dr. Hill raised an even more important issue when he asked, "Will we prove to have what it takes to make those leaders great?"

No leader can be effective beyond the willingness of people to follow and support him. Leadership, it has been said, purely and simply, is influence. And this is exactly what Pastor E.V. Hill was getting at. Making leaders great is the ability to help one increase his or her influence and then support them in sustaining that influence over an extended period of time.

So while we speak of the need for a unifying and igniting vision, we must think through the leadership factor and ask ourselves, if we are prepared to "make great" leaders among us. The key word is "among us." Why? Because it is much easier to follow those who are either no longer here or those we do not know.

THE NECESSARY TRAITS

So what will you do concerning these matters? First, I am asking you to think about this seriously—because the future of the race depends on leadership.

Second, begin to identify those around you who have such traits. Be careful and prayerful here. Before elevating someone to a higher level of leadership, evaluate their past performance because we tend to be swayed by the things some imposters practice and do, and therefore we end up empowering people to lead who have no fruitful place to take us.

Consider these insights to use in the evaluation process:

Character: Look for honesty and integrity. Are they truthful? How well do they manage? Have they overcome whatever flaws they have?

Caring: How deeply do they care about the group? How has this been evidenced?

Competence: Are they a student of the situation? Do they have a real grasp of the problems and solutions?

Commitment: Have you seen a willingness to make personal sacrifices for the sake of the whole?

Courage: How have they handled opposition in the past? Has there been a demonstration of courage? Are they willing to stand with the right minority against the wrong majority?

This generation often makes the mistake of valuing cosmetics and clothes over the qualities we have just mentioned. We tend to place volume over vision and consequently, people who are dressed up and talking loud, win our support too easily. There is a need for better discernment and judgment.

THE NEXT LEVEL

One of the reasons the hip hop culture expresses such disdain for African American leaders of our day is because they are discerning enough to see how cowardly and selfishly we have behaved. They see that, up until now, we have been unwilling to continue the movement which, for the most part, died with Dr. King and his generation. The laws which were changed and programs established were intended to create a climate for the continuance of our united progress. Instead, too many of us became intoxicated with individual increase. The hip hop crowd has a right to be angry. And while I disagree with their manner of expression, I understand their bitterness. They feel they have not only been betrayed by the white power establishment, but also by the black leading class. This is why they are suspicious and cynical towards black leaders, including preachers and elected persons.

Anytime rights are established, responsibilities have to be clearly defined and adhered to—this is where we have to go to get back on track. It is now our obligation to use our legal rights, our insight gained through exposure and education, our wisdom gained through experience, our relationships gained through integration and faith gained through seeing God work, to take our movement to the next level and our people into a new dimension. The goal was never for us to get here and die. In our vernacular, "The devil is a liar."

The black middle and elite classes cannot give enough lip service to change this perception. The only hope is for something substantive to be done which will unify our people at the neighborhood level. This movement should include, but is clearly not limited to, economic empowerment.

Different from earlier generations of blacks, this group

169

understands the need to make money, build wealth and will respect you only if you agree. This may be a fault, but the point is, they can handle and embrace leaders with some cash. The problem they have is with those who are only interested in their *personal* bottom line and who could care less about the rest of the community.

A CULTURE-WIDE CHANGE

It is probably clear, but let me state it concisely. I am not advocating a charitable program, not calling on those mentioned earlier and others to merely donate their time, money and energy to saving our community. To the contrary, I am asking them to invest with our community, encourage others to do so and to expect dividends in the process.

In turn, it would be *expected* for blacks to respond to their willingness to invest in such a vision by supporting the Empowerment Villages by moving within them, locating their businesses there and of course, trading their discretionary dollars in these places as much as possible.

I perfectly understand this demands a culture-wide change in mindset. This is why throughout the book, I advocate one simple and profound philosophy: *empower those who empower us.* Any other practice is foolish and reveals self-hatred or a lack of self-love and self esteem. The problem is, as Brother Kunjufu points out, blacks earn $688 billion annually and only spend 4% of this money with black-owned businesses.

With our gross annual revenue, it is unexplainable for us not to be better off. Yes, we could certainly afford to increase our wealth, but we must change our mentality about how we spend our capital.

At some point, we have to understand that you produce black millionaires by creating black billionaires. A sound and growing elite class should result in a growing middle class. This is the way it has and continually works in other communities, and it is the only plan which will work for us. Let me be blunt: equal opportunity will never be a reality where there is not equal control—which is why we are always fighting for it. As we generate wealth in the black community, we gain the power to provide more viable opportunities for our own sons and daughters.

This is why the mentality I advocate is so critical. Tavis Smiley expresses it when he proclaims, "Think black first." Marcus Garvey believed in it. And, before Revlon, Maybelline and Max Factor, we also believed. This is how Madame C. J. Walker became the first African American millionaire, selling her hair products across the country and employing hundreds of representatives. Thinking opposite of this has caused many black-owned businesses to fail.

We need a strategy designed to increase the 4% to 7%, 10%, 15% and 20% over a prescribed period of time. Presently, we spend our dollars with others and our change with black owned businesses and firms.

When we built our new multimillion dollar sanctuary facility (The King's Dome), our lead construction team was majority black. People still marvel that first we were *willing* to do it and second we found blacks *able* to do it. Our project stands today as a model of what we can do when given the opportunity. Hopefully, this will encourage and help someone else to change.

IT'S JOSHUA'S TIME

After Moses, the great and unmatched emancipator of the Israelites died, God immediately raised up new leadership to whom was given a Promise Land vision. *"Then God spoke to Joshua, son of Nun, who had been Moses' servant (and student), saying, Moses my servant is dead, now therefore arise, cross this Jordan, you and all these people, to the land that I am giving to them...Be strong and courageous, for you will give this people possession of the land which I swore to give to them."*

The question we face is, "Who are the Joshua's of our day?" Joshua was not Moses and whomever we have to lead us will not be Martin King. There will certainly be some similarities but not a replica. Anointing is always "assignment specific" and "time limited." Moses' anointing was for crossing the Red Sea and wilderness survival. Joshua's anointing was for crossing the Jordan River and Promise Land conquering.

Dr. King's anointing was for his assignment in his season. All those who were connected to him shared in that anointing and experienced favor. But now that we are in the 21st century, facing giants we have never seen who are set to block us from our new dimension destiny, we need living leadership with vision and courage to conquer new territory.

Those around Joshua discerned his special traits, perceived his purpose and embraced his position among them. And they answered Joshua saying, *"All you instructed us to do we will do it, and wherever you direct us we will go...Who ever rebels (rises) to undermine you will be eliminated."* This was the caliber of leader-followers who stood with Joshua and that is why he became so effective.

Those who supported him had what it took to make a leader great:

- They followed him, meaning they were leadable.
- They were faithful to him, meaning they were loyal.
- They fought with and for him, meaning they too were wholeheartedly committed.

Without a visionary leader there was no way to reach their collective destiny.

WHO WILL WE RECOGNIZE?

At the 2007, Stellar Gospel Music Awards held in Nashville, minister and music genius Kirk Franklin gave an unplanned message which was spoken under the power of an obvious anointing. I am grateful to have been present to hear it. Kirk challenged the event organizers, the molders and shapers of the gospel music industry and the artists to (in my words) "turn the page." He agreed with the need to remember great artists from the past but sharply warned that you can get stuck there.

Franklin admonished us to accept the fact there were new leaders on the scene today who are committed to the true cause and it is now time to recognize and embrace them. On the stage that night were certainly worthy representations of this in the persons of

Tye Tribbet, Donald Lawrence, Mary Mary and of course, Kirk Franklin. He reminded us that defeating the demons we now face requires the gifts and anointing that this generation's leaders in the industry possess.

I have challenged audiences for years on the same subject. Our hero, Dr. Martin Luther King, Jr., came, served, led, sacrificed and made changes which continue to bless us today. But we have to accept the fact—he is gone. We can no longer look to him for leadership or a vision. We can respect, remember and be inspired by him, but we cannot follow him.

I advocate a principle I encourage you to embrace: "Never treat the uncommon as though it is common." My spiritual leader and mentor, Dr. Samuel Jackson Gilbert, Sr., says "Gold is gold, even if it is in your own backyard." God has probably placed a visionary close to you.

WE CAN RISE, BUT WE MUST UNITE

Without question, implementing the unity principles is the key to the future of the black community, and for that matter, blacks around the world. It is irrational to think otherwise. Whatever we have to get over and get beyond in order to come together, simply must happen. Of course, this means trusting, respecting, believing and loving each other. This will be hard work, but the bottom line remains, we need each other.

The fear of those who continue to take advantage of our disunity is that we will unite. The prayers of elders have always been that we would. The world actually awaits to see the marvel that will result when we arrive. This effort must be undergirded by a belief in our collective potentiality and in the confidence of such a possibility. We have to begin to speak it in the affirmative and to lift up every example when we see it.

"O how good and pleasant it is when brothers dwell together in unity. There, the Lord commands the blessing, even life forever!" (Psalm 133).

God himself is waiting to see if we will begin to break down the superficial barriers that presently divide us. Barriers such as geography, skin shade, economic status, personal achievements and denominational preferences. Have you ever eaten M&M's candy? They come in red, yellow, green, brown, orange and blue colors, but beneath the surface of each coating is chocolate. And they all taste good! This mirrors us. We are all in the same box and we are all the same beneath our thin surfaces. It's time to change our direction in the 21st century.

We cannot be healthy outside of our community before we are healthy inside our community. Let's encourage and expect our churches to unite. We should not be competitors, rather co-laborers. We must admonish our civic and elected leaders to unite; our neighborhoods are at stake. Let us work together to cement our divided genders and divided generations. Ultimately our failures and our successes are shared realities.

CHAPTER NINE

IS THERE HOPE?

We need a generation of prophets and leaders
who will have the courage, compassion and confidence
to say to black America, "You shall live and not die!"

After reading this book, in which so much attention has been given to clearly laying out the severity of the black condition, it is possible to conclude we are already doomed! However, processing the statistical data which drives home the fact we are in a state of emergency is necessary because without it we may be unwilling to believe things are as they are—and thus not be inclined to change our behavior.

Who wants a lying doctor giving them test results? Regardless of the condition, it is better to have an accurate and honest diagnosis, no matter how painful it may be initially. Of course, immediately following a truthful report, you want to hear a prognosis that is favorable, based on an informed approach to treatment.

This is what I have attempted to do. From the beginning, I have sought to expose you to the reality of our current predicament by painting an honest picture of our present state. I must admit, however, it has caused me anguish to re-read, analyze and process these negative reports and facts. Maybe you have felt the same. Perhaps you are deeply disturbed, even angry—wondering whether or not our situation can be turned around. Is there hope?

To answer this question, it was necessary to look to a source beyond my human capacity to reason and predict. I sought the omniscient God who created all people because I know He never guesses. For He alone looks on the future and sees it as the completed past. So, I wanted to know from Him, where are we headed? What are our chances? Can we and will we overcome? Is there any legitimate reason to fight on? Should I continue to challenge African Americans in the words of Jesse Jackson, to "Keep Hope Alive"?

The answers to my questions came from an infallible source and provided the inspiration and instruction I needed to continue believing in our collective victorious destiny. Remember, the question is not, "Can I make it?" It is, "Can WE make it?"

There is a story recorded in the Book of Ezekiel, Chapter 37, in the Old Testament, I would encourage you to take a few minutes to read. I believe it to be the divine response to the black predicament at the beginning of the 21st century.

A GHASTLY SIGHT

The prophet Ezekiel shares a vision in which the hand of the Lord led him out into a valley and sat him down in the middle of a wasteland which was filled with dry bones. These were the skeletal remains of a people who were once vibrant, vivacious, and victorious. But now, all that was left were dismembered remnants of frail, fractured parts of body frames—bitter reminders of a people who once existed as a mighty force. The place to which he was led was a mass open grave.

As you can imagine this was a ghastly sight; an entire valley filled with bones. It was enough to turn one's stomach. I know well that feeling, and perhaps you do too:

- I get it whenever I visit the projects and see my sisters with multiple children struggling to make sense of poverty.
- I get it when I look into the eyes of boys and girls, who due

to no fault of their own, are living in filth, wearing hand-me-down clothes, existing in dope-infested quarters in the shadows of a downtown multi-million-dollar skyline.

- I get the feeling when I visit a publicly funded hospital where the uninsured are packed in emergency rooms waiting for substandard care, knowing my insurance card is safe in my wallet.
- I get that sick feeling when I see my homeless brothers and sisters, many of whom are mentally ill, eating from trash cans, begging for coins and smelling of body waste.
- And yes, I get that queasy feeling in my stomach when I encounter students who can't read or write at age 13—knowing they are likely destined to the penitentiary.
- I also get it when I visit a jail or prison unit and witness caged humanity under the authority of the state.

Each of these are ghastly sights for me.

A GRASP OF THE SITUATION

Next, Ezekiel informs us he was led to walk around in the valley, getting close enough to the bones so they would not appear to him as one large pile of lifeless matter. Rather, he was made to come so near he could observe them individually. In order to truly appreciate the situation, Ezekiel had to examine, process, see and smell those bones up close and personal. It must have been gut-wrenching. The exercise was necessary; however, because it gave this servant of God, who was to be a change agent, a real grasp of what was taking place.

This is precisely what too many of today's so-called leaders and messengers have been unwilling to do. They have not actually touched the problem. As a result they are not personally familiar with the sight, sound or smell of the suffering. There are countless ministers, politicians, professors and middle class intellectuals who never visit an inner city school, a housing project, a juvenile detention center, a homeless shelter or a street corner. Yet, these are the very persons who have elaborate well-articulated, passionate opinions about what is wrong and how it should be remedied.

I strongly admonish those who desire to be taken seriously and who intend to be effective to follow Ezekiel's model. Come down and walk around in the midst of the problem. Flying over it, driving through it with your windows up, reading about it in the local newspaper or watching cop shows on television will not suffice. There is no substitute for the <u>power of proximity.</u> We must have compassion, conviction and a compelling urge to contribute to the conversion of sisters and brothers in peril, but you cannot transform what you have never touched. You cannot heal what you refuse to handle. You cannot speak to what you have not listened to. The Christ example is the best. He became what we are so that we might become what He is.

GROUP CIRCUMSTANCE

There are still too many blacks who strive to ignore our plural concerns, choosing to operate in denial of our unbreakable linkage. They remain insensitive to the insights that confirm our inextricable connectedness. So they read unrelated books, watch unrelated TV shows and movies, attend other people's functions, preach other people's sermons and keep the socially relevant matters regarding black culture off the agendas they control.

I believe it is time for us to open our minds and understand that the misery of the multitude will eventually engulf us all if the situation goes unaddressed.

In the valley of dry bones which Ezekiel explored, there were no superficial distinctions. Those which had existed before tragedy and annihilation struck, were now no longer visible or relevant. This is also true for blacks in America and in the world. A careful and calculated analysis would reveal that our circumstances are not truly singular. Rather, our predicament is plural. Those who are reliant on personal positions and power are greatly deceived. We had better begin to think on the intricacies pertaining to group destiny. Any other premise is faulty and flawed and will prove fatal. We are all too connected to believe we can succeed without each other:

- As long as over one million black men are in prison, we are locked up.
- As long as the larger percentages of AIDS cases are blacks in America and Africa, we are dying of the disease.
- As long as the unemployment rate for blacks is double that of whites, we are not working.
- As long as most black schools are segregated, under-funded and under-performing, we are eroding intellectually.
- As long as unjust policies pigeon-hole the poor, we are all discriminated against.

It is a group circumstance because if current trends continue, we all end up in the mass grave which has already been dug for us. There, only bones remain. In the final analysis, there is no way to distinguish which used to be bones of the educated or uneducated; or which were formerly bones of the lower, middle or elite classes; or which bones came from the hood or the suburbs; or which bones voted Democrat or Republican; or which were Baptist or Pentecostal. In the end, no matter what their prior state of grief or glory, they all were united in the same burial place and had all things in common; station, status and stench.

THE QUESTION IS...

After completing a thorough survey of the situation, the prophet Ezekiel is then asked to give his personal prognosis: "Can these bones live?"

That is the question God posed to him and it is the essential issue with which we are confronted at the outset of this century. This is the same question blacks faced in the 19th and 20th centuries. Frederick Douglass and his contemporaries faced it. DuBois and Washington faced it. It was dealt with again by Martin and Malcolm. And it is asked once more of us today.

Before, it was, "Can these Negroes...?" then, "Can these colored's...?" then, "Can these blacks..?" now, "Can these African Americans live?"

It must be noted that while the labels we have worn have

changed, we are not a different people. We act a little different, but we are the same group. The contents are within the container, not in the external label. Let us be clear: we are the same people we have always been and we are special in the heart of God.

So the question before us is, "Can these bones live?" In other words, can these who have failed educationally, fluttered politically, faltered economically, are flawed morally, feeble medically, unfaithful spiritually—can they come to life again?

- Although they are in dire straights according to every major indicator, are statistically on the bottom and others are laughing at them, can they live?
- Although the doomsayers have already pronounced them dead and done, can they live?
- Although sociological experts have forecasted that their fate is final and the word on the street is that other minorities have been chosen to replace them, the question being debated and discussed in the hood and in the university is, "Can they live?"

Ezekiel's response reveals the overwhelming perplexity in which he found himself. There were no visible and intelligible signs of life. However, he was in the presence of God; and because he was in a conversation with the Author of life, he could not dare answer according to his limited senses. Thus, he wisely responded. "Lord, you know the answer."

DO YOU REALLY BELIEVE?

Those who have had a hand in developing sinister schemes and poisonous policies look at us and declare, "They cannot live." Those who have hoped for our demise and participated in our peril by default are making the same prediction.

This is like a boxer who has absorbed blow after blow, some legal punches and others illegally thrown while the referee looks the other way. Finally, the battered boxer collapses on the canvass. Now, the crowd silently waits while the official count is made.

Those who bet against the fallen warrior lick their chops, as does the unscrupulous opponent, anticipating the ill-earned spoils. But until the final bell rings the question remains, "Can he live?" And this is the question put to Ezekiel by God, "Do you believe these bones can live?"

Tragically, many blacks have become fatalistic in their thinking, having given up on our chances. Those with this view have consciously decided to abandon the group, claiming to have no part in our collective dilemma, neither our united destiny. They are concretely convinced that as a people we are done with; they support no black causes and join no efforts aimed at addressing any aspect of the black condition. They also intentionally tune out any voice which seeks to inform black consciousness and lift our expectations. Today, I come to say to this group of fatalists, this response is premature and quite presumptuous.

What happens next in the valley of dry bones is crucial as the prophet is instructed to prophesy—to proclaim a Word to these skeletal remains. The message Ezekiel proclaimed was that God was going to revive, restore, resurrect and reposition those lifeless bones. But none of this would occur unless they would hear the Word of the Lord. Their life would be in the Word.

Therefore, Ezekiel is charged to speak truth to power—to a group (bones) that appeared to have no possibility in them; a group which seemed to be forever drained of potential; a group upon whom death had already been legally, educationally, medically and economically pronounced. But yet he spoke, and he spoke in faith.

FORTITUDE AND FAITH

This takes courage because those who are willing to speak life in the midst of death are always in the minority. Most do not have the gumption to do so—and those who dare are criticized by shallow prognosticators. They run the risk of being labeled out of step with the times and out of touch with reality. Speaking prophetically in the midst of tragedy also takes confidence, being fully persuaded that the part you play will make a difference.

This is an hour for leaders who have fortitude and faith. Fortitude to look squarely at the situation and say with gusto, "We will overcome, we will rise again!" Faith looks not to the past but to the future. It is the *"the substance of things hoped for, the evidence of things not seen."* Here is how I choose to explain it: "Faith is an uncompromising confidence in God's ability to perform His perfect will on your behalf, no matter what the opposition." Fortitude is the boldness to pursue a thing that is unpopular and unsupported.

HOPE FOR THE FUTURE

Speaking truth to power is the assignment for those called to lead in the restoration of black America. Those who receive our message must catch it, believe it and act accordingly. The passage tells us that upon hearing this word of possibility, a noise was heard in the valley and the bones began to resonate with the proclamation of life. It seemed they had been waiting on a Word which declared to them in faith, they had a future ahead of them—and this is what this generation desperately needs to hear. No more negativity.

Here is the Word for us in this hour: *"'For I know the plans I have for you,' declares the Lord, 'plans to prosper you and not to harm you, plans to give you hope and a future'"* (Jeremiah 29:11). It is the Divine will for us to live, prosper and succeed. In other words, "We are not going out like this!"

Then, the bones began to come together (Ezekiel 37:7). They were joined bone to bone as each one took its appropriate place. There it is—UNITY!

In our context this means that the home, the church and the school must be reconnected. When this happens our elected officials and business community must and *will* come together. As our spiritual, familial, intellectual, financial and political pieces all unite, we will be well and whole.

Once all the bones were connected and covered with skin, the Spirit came and breathed new life into them. The very essence of God caused them to come alive.

Please understand, we must believe again as a people that life is not in the abundance of material goods. It is in God. "In Him we live, move and have our being." With Him, "all things are possible, and without Him, we can do nothing." My grandmother believed this, and so do I. And our unborn grandchildren must understand it as well. So pass it on.

RISE UP!

Finally, as Ezekiel prophesied, those bones, "*...stood up upon their feet, an exceeding great army*" (v.10).

By speaking truth to power, we will bring that which is dead back to life—they will have the desire and the will to rise up! This is a picture of independence and self sufficiency. It is also symbolic of dignity.

In this century, blacks will once again stand on our own feet. We will rise up to be a liberated, educated, economically viable, wealthy, healthy people. We will be an army, ready to fight to defend our own, protect our territory and take what rightfully belongs to us and to help build an America that the world truly admires.

So...

- The next time you see a news story reporting a tragedy involving blacks, say, "These bones can live."
- The next time you see a young brother with sagging pants and his underwear showing, declare, "These bones can live!"
- The next time you see an unwed pregnant teenage girl, proclaim, "These bones can live!"
- The next time you drive through the projects and witness the burden of blight, shout out, "These bones can live!"
- The next time you encounter a black elitist who has disowned their blackness, proclaim, "These bones can live!"
- The next time you visit a black church and observe no signs of Afro-sensitivity, utter the words, "These bones can live!"

- The next time you see a policeman arresting a black youth on the side of the street, say with conviction, "These bones can live!"
- The next time you see blacks and whites at odds, say it: "These bones can live!"

When you fall on your knees tonight please pray, "God, you are good all the time, and because you are, I believe these bones will live!"

Yes, there is hope!

CHAPTER TEN

WHAT WE CAN DO

No one can do everything,
but everyone can do something!

Looking at the present predicament of black America with natural eyes, it would be easy to throw in the towel and give up. But we serve a supernatural God—who expects His people to turn what is ordinary into something extraordinary.

Personally, I am excited to be living in a generation that has the potential to restore our people to the place of honor, dignity and respect which is their destiny.

This brings us to the question, "What can we do?"—as individuals and collectively. There are literally hundreds of actions we can take to turn the situation around, but let me suggest these in particular:

- In every city, blacks should produce a Heritage Calendar and on the birthdays of legendary blacks, there ought to be celebrations in homes, etc.
- Every black church must begin teaching financial responsibility as a part of its empowerment curriculum.
- Black leaders in business, religion, politics, social activism and entertainment should declare a moratorium on frivolous spending.

185

- We must discontinue complimenting people solely for their apparel. Instead, we need to express admiration for their natural, God-given beauty, true achievement, performance and productivity. By doing this, we will destroy the myth that things (clothes and jewelry) make us attractive and we will begin to value the characteristics which are truly significant.
- We need to stop buying clothing purely for the purpose of dressing to impress. This will send a strong message to manufacturers, retailers and advertisers that we are no longer an impulsive, gullible market.
- Preachers, athletes and other key people of influence should commit to wearing modest apparel more often. Church members need to be given permission and instruction on how to dress, "Christian casual." It is about worship, not "wear-ship."
- We must promote professional black athletes such as NBA superstar Stefan Marberry who introduced a lowcost brand of tennis shoes—publicly expressing his concern and conviction regarding the over-priced footwear black athletes are paid millions to sell to black children and parents who can least afford them. Other athletes should be encouraged to join him or foster similar acts.
- All black organizations, institutions and leaders must unite to publicize the slogan "Black Is Beautiful." The purpose being to dispel the notion of black inferiority and to promote self-esteem, respect and appreciation.
- In every African American community, the message must be emphasized for all parents to be engaged in their children's education. We cannot afford to produce another generation of anti-intellectuals who become parents themselves, continuing the cycle.
- We must promote academics over athletics.
- It is time to reclaim our heritage of honest, character-building hard work.

- Going to jail must no longer be seen as a badge of honor or a "rite of passage" into manhood.
- There must be consequences for crime, yet blatant injustices within our system must be vigorously challenged.
- Put privately run prisons out of business by not going to jail.
- Blow the whistle on corporations who use prison labor to lower production costs—and are causing prisons to look more and more like slavery plantations.
- Companies that profit from prison labor must be mandated to hire ex-felons.
- Parents must accept the responsibility of knowing and caring where their children are, who they are with, what they are doing and the associated consequences.
- Launch organizations, city by city, to stand up against the debased image of black women portrayed on TV screens and in the lyrics of music.
- African American parents must become aggressive in educating and protecting their kids regarding sexual matters. Being timid discussing these issues is not an acceptable excuse.
- Today's black church must accept the responsibility of leading our community to make a turn-around and once again create a powerful new wave of progress in black America.
- Every black church needs to have some form of HIV/AIDS ministry.
- We need an "empowerment theology" which explains our history, defines our identity and clarifies our destiny. It would reveal we are a peculiar people of noble purpose among our fellow man. It would demand values-based character and social responsibility which elevates the race and contributes to the progression of humanity.
- Look for people with whom to unite who are dedicated to saving our community, whether they are African Americans or not.

- Empower those who empower us and reject those who do not. Join people and organizations that are sensitive and serious concerning our plight.
- We must accept the responsibility of leaving a legacy of spiritual, intellectual and material wealth.
- It's time to envision our race building and controlling markets. For example, not just buying gasoline, but producing and distributing energy resources.
- We need a vision and strategic plan for creating Black Empowerment Districts (Villages) in every major city in America. These districts should become economic engines which grow existing entrepreneurs, create new ones, and redevelop and resurrect run-down sections of our communities that once thrived.
- Today, we need to identify, recognize and embrace black visionary leaders within our midst.
- We must emphasize career building, not just job training.
- Black leadership from all walks of life—including entertainment, sports, education, government and the church—need to come together as a unified force to restore the black community.
- Make sure everyone in your circle of contacts knows you are reading this book and find a way to discuss its contents.
- Share this message with every student, parent, preacher, teacher, elected official, business person, hip hop artist, athlete and entertainer you know. In our case, ignorance is not bliss; it is deadly!

You may not be able to tackle each of these issues, but you can do *something* to make a difference. Together, however, we can bring about a mighty change.

It is my prayer that one day soon we will no longer be asking, "Why are blacks doing so bad?"

With good people, assisted by a good God, our vision will become a reality.

RESOURCES AND RECOMMENDED READING

Anderson, Claud, PowerNomics: *The National Plan to Empower Black America,* Bethesda, MD: PowerNomics Corporation of America, 2001.

Cone, James, *Malcolm and Martin in America: A Dream or a Nightmare,* Maryknoll, NY: Orbis Books, 1992.

Crane, Dianna, *Fashion and Its Social Agendas: Class, Gender, and Identity in Clothing,* Chicago, IL: University of Chicago Press, 2001.

Dixon, James II, *The Difference is Vision,* Houston, TX: JD II Publishing Company, Inc., 2004.

Dobson, James, Parenting Isn't for Cowards, Word Publishing Group, Nashville, TN, 1988.

Dyson, Michael E., *Is Bill Cosby Right? Or Has the Black Middle Class Lost It's Mind,* New York, NY: Basic Civitas Books, 2006.

Hacker, Andrew, *Two Nations: Black and White, Separate, Hostile.* New York, NY: Simon & Schuster, 1992.

King, J. L., *On The Down Low: A Journey into the Lives of "Straight" Men Who Sleep With Men,* New York, NY: Broadway Books, 2004.

Kitwana, Bakari, *The Hip Hop Generation: Young Blacks and the Crisis in African American Culture,* New York, NY: Basic Civitas Books, 2002.

Kunjufu, Jawanza, *Solutions for Black America,* Chicago, IL: African American Images, 2004.

Larson, Erik V., *Isaac's Storm,* New York, NY: Random House, 1999.

Roberts, Michael V., *Action Has No Season,* Bloomington, IN: AuthorHouse Publishing, 2005.

Smiley, Tavis, The Covenant with Black America, Chicago, IL: Third World Press, 2006.

Steffans, Karrine, *Confessions of a Video Vixen,* New York, NY: Harper Collins Publishers, 2005.

Williams, Juan, *Enough.* New York, NY: Random House, Inc., 2006.

Woodson, Carter G., *The Mis-Education of the Negro,* Trenton, NJ: Africa World Press, 1990.

Wright, Bruce, *Black Robes, White Justice: Why Our Legal System Doesn't Work for Blacks,* New York, NY: Kensington Publishing Corporation, 2002.

JAMES DIXON SPEAKS!

FOR SCHEDULING CALL OR EMAIL:

(713) 688-2900 OR crystalj@clearsail.net

INTERNET: www.cofempowers.org

FOLLOW JAMES DIXON ON TWITTER: @BishopJDixon
AND ON FACEBOOK AT: James Dixon, II

JAMES DIXON, II
P.O. BOX 924083
HOUSTON, TX 77292